ADMISSIBLE
EVIDENCE

CREATION SCIENCE IN A
MODERN-DAY SCOPES TRIAL

by

DR. JOHN L. DOANE

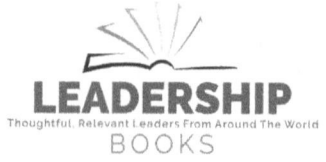

LEADERSHIP
Thoughtful, Relevant Leaders From Around The World
BOOKS

To Merrill A. Cohen, MD

ACKNOWLEDGMENTS

First of all, I am thankful to *The Christian Post* for publishing several of my opinion pieces online. That experience led to a relationship with Leadership Books, the publishing affiliate of *The Christian Post*. The staff at Leadership Books has been instrumental both in the genesis and execution of this book. First of all, the intake editor reviewed my previous book and noted its textbook-like style. He suggested a more appealing format that led me to adopt a trial transcript and personalize the story as a way of conveying the important information in the present book.

The trial format has the added advantage of presenting opposing views in a simple and easy-to-follow manner. In bringing a story to life, I considered the all-too-realistic possibility of a science teacher fired from his job, which allowed for additional commentary and personality. Thanks to my Executive Editor who expertly transposed the draft manuscript into a readable narrative while adding human interest and style. I hope your understanding is enriched in the pages of this book as you consider the merits of creation science.

ENDORSEMENTS

"I love this. It is a great idea for a book. Well done!"

Dr. Timothy Clarey
Director of Research
Institute for Creation Research

*****

"I realized that you were trying to keep the testimonies simple so readers could understand...I think you have done a very reasonable job of accomplishing that."

Dr. Andrew Snelling
Contract Research Geologist,
Answers in Genesis (USA)

*****

"I've looked over all the sections about my research. They are very accurate and amazingly so. You did a good job of it."

Dr. D. Russell Humphreys
Physicist and Author

*****

"Valuing the truth and having a heart for the upcoming generations, I have found *Admissible Evidence* to be a great tool of support that links God's word to scientific research. Admissible Evidence brings this link to life in a tangible way for people of all ages and backgrounds to grow and enjoy; Great Work!"

Pastor Emilian Mihet
Grandview Baptist Church,
Anchorage, AK

*****

"*Admissible Evidence* gives us all the evidence that we wish the Scopes Trial 100 years ago had used to stem the tide of evolutionary secularism. In 2025, the creationists are finally in their prime!"

Ed Kalish, M.T.S.
Nashotah House Theological Seminary
Priest Emeritus, Traditional Anglican Church

TABLE OF CONTENTS

MONDAY

TUESDAY

WEDNESDAY

WED   THURSDAY   FRIDAY

SAT

SUN

MON

TUE

CAST OF CHARACTERS

- Jason Radcliffe, former science teacher at Branchburg High School
  - Wife Carol
  - Son Collin
- Judge Jacobsen of the Branchburg Courthouse
- Atty Brian Cardona, representing Plaintiff Jason Radcliffe
- Atty Charles Porter, representing the Branchburg School Board, the defendant in this case
- Court Clerk
- Henry Manning, Reporter for the *Branchburg Times*
- Douglas Thomason, Reporter for the *Dale County News-Register*
- Brandon Taylor, friend of the Radcliffes and Brian Cardona
- Peter Benson and Stuart Donner, two of Jason Radcliffe's former students
- Dr. Jackie Kennard, principal of Branchburg High School
- Pastor Dan, Jason Radcliffe's Pastor at Branchburg Church of the Open Door

LIST OF WITNESSES

- Witness 1, representing the work of Louis Pasteur
- Witness 2, representing the work of Stanley Miller
- Witness 3, representing the work of Charles Darwin
- Witness 4, representing the work of John Sanford
- Witness 5, representing the work of Nathaniel Jeanson and Jeffrey Tomkins
- Witness 6, representing the work of Dennis Venema
- Witness 7, representing the work of John Morris and Frank Sherwin
- Witness 8, representing the work of Steve Austin, Tim Clarey, Andrew Snelling, John Whitmore and Ron Neller
- Witness 9, representing the work of Carol Hill, Gregg Davidson, Tim Helble and Wayne Ranney

- Witness 10, representing the work of John Baumgardner
- Witness 11, representing the work of D. Russell Humphreys
- Witness 12, representing the work of Andrew Snelling
- Witness 13, representing the work of Roger Wiens
- Witness 14, representing the work of Stephen Hawking

PROLOGUE

THE SOUTH SUDANESE ARMY BATTALION

In 2016, an army of Islamic soldiers from northern Sudan attacked the headquarters of a small unit of soldiers from South Sudan in the contested Nuba Mountain region. The South Sudanese soldiers held off the first assault, but worried that their outnumbered group would not be able to hold off a second assault. They called for Ismail, a Christian chaplain, and told him they had only one large gun and a few rounds of ammunition. Ismail came and prayed, "Lord, may every shell hit its target to protect your people." He fired the first shell, and it hit an ammunition truck, igniting it in a massive ball of fire. His second shell exploded a fuel truck. After he fired the third shell, the opposition burst into frenzied terror, consulted their witchdoctor and then fled.[1]

In the culture wars going on today we can identify two important strongholds, like the ammunition truck and the fuel truck in the above story.

The first stronghold is the claim that science must be separated from theology and the Bible, so that only scientists can know the truth about the physical origins of the earth. This claim, used in attacks on the reliability of the Biblical accounts in Genesis, is like the fuel truck. The second claim is that few, if any, serious scientists believe in evidence that the earth is young. This second claim, used in similar attacks, is like the ammunition truck.

Without the fuel to bring weapons close to the South Sudanese outpost, those weapons would have been ineffective at long distance. Similarly, it would be easier to defend the reliability of Genesis on theological grounds if the first "fuel truck" claim were false, even if the second claim were true. On the other hand, getting weapons near the outpost using fuel in trucks would be useless without the ammunition for those weapons. If accredited creation scientists actually exist – counter to the second "ammunition truck" claim – they could counter false assertions from non-Christian scientists.

Just as Islam helped motivate the soldiers manning the ammunition truck and fuel truck against the South Sudanese soldiers, it should not be surprising that religious motives lie behind many people making the culture war claims mentioned above. We find ourselves involved not simply in a conflict between science and religion; we find ourselves in a spiritual battle. We do not fight against "flesh and blood," as Paul writes in Ephesians 6:12; and the weapons of our warfare are also not carnal (of flesh and blood) but are mighty in God for pulling down strongholds (see 2 Corinthians 10:4).

Join us in the following pages, where you will witness a similar battle as it plays out in the case of a trial concerning the admissibility and believability of evidence from creation science. The courtroom setting highlights the forensic nature of questions about origins.[2]

MONDAY MORNING

THE OFFICE OF ATTORNEY BRIAN CARDONA

In the town of Branchburg Tennessee, Jason Radcliffe sat and listened to his attorney Brian Cardona in his office. The young man looked to be in his late twenties and ran his fingers through his thick black hair. He seemed apprehensive and looked around intermittently as if unsure what his attorney, Brian Cardona, had been saying.

"Jason, don't you remember when I told you the story about the South Sudanese soldiers? Don't you think that God could help us here also?"

Jason looked up and asked, "Do you really think I could get my job back? It's already been six months since the school district fired me."

"They really did fire you unjustly," Brian remarked. "And something pretty similar happened elsewhere, so it's important that the judge send a clear message in his verdict, so it doesn't continue to happen to others."[3]

He went over his plan for the trial one more time. "We first need to get the judge to allow our evidence to be presented. When that's done, we have plenty of expert witnesses who can carry the day. The judge will have to agree that the books you had in your science classroom library were acceptable supplementary material."

Jason thought that this seemed hopeful, but wondered if his school and students would welcome him back. He also worried if enough friends and well-wishers would continue supporting his crowdfunded legal fund. "Mr. Cardona, are you sure you want to go forward with this? I don't know if I'll have enough funds to carry it through to the end."

"Enough of that right now. And please, call me Brian." He stopped pacing and sat down across from Jason. "This afternoon I need to go before the judge and argue with Attorney Porter about a pre-trial motion he submitted. You should be there with me. That'll no doubt take up the afternoon.

"You'll also need to be in the courtroom in the morning in case the formal trial starts then. Let's meet in the courthouse cafeteria around eight in the morning."

"That reminds me," Jason remarked. "My wife Carol wants to bring our four-year-old son, Collin, to see me testify. Would that be okay?"

"Do you think Collin can stay quiet?"

"Well, we've been keeping him with us in church services and he's been pretty good there."

"Okay," Brian replied, "have him and your wife come by around 9:30. We have opening statements first – before your testimony."

"By the way, are the expert witnesses in town?" Jason asked.

"I briefed the first ones Saturday," Brian responded. "They are staying at the Overlook Hotel. The others are coming on Tuesday evening or Wednesday morning."

MONDAY AFTERNOON

A COURTROOM IN THE BRANCHBURG COURTHOUSE

The Trial Setting

JUDGE JACOBSEN "Good afternoon. Will the attorneys present introduce themselves."

ATTY CARDONA "I am Brian Cardona, representing the plaintiff Jason Radcliffe."

ATTY PORTER "I am Charles Porter, representing the Branchburg school board, the defendant in this case."

JUDGE JACOBSEN "All right. Will the clerk state the summary of this case?"

CLERK "The Branchburg school board relieved former science teacher Jason Radcliffe of his job last October when it was alleged that he had placed unsuitable creation science books in the library of his classroom at Branchburg High School. Teacher Radcliffe claims that he was unlawfully dismissed and requests relief from this Court to require the school board to reinstate him as science teacher."

JUDGE JACOBSEN "Are any monetary damages claimed by the plaintiff?"

CLERK "No."

JUDGE JACOBSEN "In that case, this will be a bench trial not requiring a jury."

PRE-TRIAL MOTIONS

Is Creation Science Religious

JUDGE JACOBSEN "Mr. Porter, I understand that you filed a motion to dismiss."

ATTY PORTER "Yes, your honor, I move that this case be dismissed based on precedent. For example, on December 20, 2005, federal Judge John E. Jones III issued a decision that marked the end of the case of *Kitzmiller vs Dover Area School District*.[4] The school board in that Pennsylvania district had mandated that intelligent design be cited as an alternative to evolution.

"Judge Jones stated that intelligent design violates 'the ground rules of science' by making allowance for the existence of the supernatural, adding that 'since the scientific revolution of the 16th and 17th centuries, science has been limited to the search for natural causes to explain natural phenomena.' The Genesis account, like intelligent design, describes allegedly supernatural causes. Therefore, all references to the religious book of Genesis are not allowed in science classes."

JUDGE JACOBSEN "Mr. Cardona, do you wish to make a response?"

ATTY CARDONA "Yes, your honor."

JUDGE JACOBSEN "All right, Mr. Cardona, proceed with your response."

ATTY CARDONA "Allow me to observe that the first one to assert specifically that science must be separated from theology and the Bible was Baruch Spinoza in the 17th century.[5] Spinoza was an apostate Jewish philosopher who had his own religion. He is generally identified as a pantheist because he equated God with Nature.

"He denied the supernatural and believed that progress and possibly a vague love for one's neighbor were principles behind Nature. Those are pantheistic beliefs. Spinoza's ideas were not only very influential in the Enlightenment but, as well-known historian Jonathan Israel has observed, those ideas inspired ideas about evolution.[6]

"Judge Jones' claim that science is limited to the search for natural causes to explain natural phenomena is itself a truth claim. Truth claims are inherently religious, and pantheism is the religion behind that claim. To exclude the Bible from considerations of science is to assert that pantheistic religion takes precedent over Biblical religion."

ATTY PORTER "We should accept the overwhelming consensus of secular scientists today, such as popular astrophysicist Stephen Hawking. He stated, 'There is a fundamental difference between religion, which is based on authority, [and] science, which is based on observation and reason. Science will win because it works.'"[7]

ATTY CARDONA "Secularism today, however, is very religious. In a speech at Notre Dame in 2019, former Attorney General William Barr observed that 'Secularists, and their allies among the "progressives," have marshaled all the force of mass communications, popular culture, the entertainment industry, and academia in an unremitting assault on religion and traditional values.' He went on to note, 'the secular project has itself become a religion, pursued with religious fervor.'"[8]

ATTY PORTER "I disagree with Barr's assessment. Consider the book, *good Without God: What a Billion Non-Religious People* Do *Believe*, written by the secular humanist chaplain at Harvard, Greg Epstein. Barr may be upset with the culture, but humanism is not a religion."

ATTY CARDONA "Epstein in fact does have a religion, it is just not a theistic religion. In his book he wrote approvingly as follows about Baruch Spinoza, for example: 'He [Spinoza] was arguably the first public Humanist in modern Western history.'[9] I mentioned already that Spinoza was very religious.

"Even Einstein considered himself a disciple of Spinoza, and wrote 'I believe in Spinoza's God, who reveals himself in the harmony of all that exists, not in a God who concerns himself with the fate and the doings of mankind.'[10]

"Then Stephen Hawking said, 'I use the word "God" in an impersonal sense, like Einstein did, so knowing the mind of God is knowing the laws of nature.'[11] The common secularism of Einstein, Hawking and Epstein is merely an expression of pantheism. The label 'secularist' is deceptive insofar as it suggests a non-religious view."

ATTY PORTER "Consider then even Francis Bacon, the Christian who some consider a leading founder of modern science. Bacon also warned against using the Bible to make theories about the natural world. In particular, he criticized those who pretended 'to find the truth of all-natural philosophy in the Scriptures; scandalizing and traducing all other philosophy as heathenish and profane.'[12, 13] By natural philosophy, Bacon of course meant what we now simply call science."

ATTY CARDONA "In fact, Bacon quoted several passages from the Bible indicating revelation about the physical world. In particular, he wrote '…likewise in that excellent Book of Job, if it be revolved with diligence, it will be found pregnant and swelling with natural philosophy….'[14]

"For example, Bacon cited passages from Job dealing with the roundness of the earth, the North Pole, and the fixity of the stars. Bacon's concern was merely that any physical insights from the Bible should be checked by observation. I am prepared to call witnesses who can show how clues from the Bible actually led to testable scientific theories.

"And why indeed was modern science indeed founded mainly by Christians like Bacon? It is because they believed in an orderly universe whose laws do not change with time or location in space. And why would they believe that? It is because they believed in a rational Creator of the universe who does not change in time and space. The natural world is not subject to the whims of gods, as in other religions. They also believed that we are made in the image of the Creator, and so we are rational beings capable of thinking His thoughts after Him and understanding His creation. Our minds are not rearranged pond scum whose thoughts might not be reliable."

ATTY PORTER "That sounds laudable, but in fact Christians were using the Bible to promote theories that did not hold up to scientific scrutiny. Conversely, remember the hard time Galileo had to convince Christians that his observations supported Copernicus' heliocentric theory."

ATTY CARDONA "It is ironic, however, that many Christians of Galileo's time were influenced by the ideas of Aristotle that dominated the universities, just as many Christians today are influenced by ideas of evolution that dominate our universities.

"Aristotle developed theories based on how he thought nature ought to behave. Hence, he wasn't very interested in checking, for example, his erroneous idea that heavy items should fall faster than light ones. Because of what they believed to be our fallen nature inherited from Adam, Christians like Bacon insisted that conclusions about the natural world needed to be checked by experiments and observations done by one's peers."

ATTY PORTER "That is exactly how modern science works. Through reason and observation, just as Hawking mentioned. We don't need revelation from the Bible for that."

ATTY CARDONA "That is true of repeatable events in the present, such as those observed by Galileo. When scientists attempt to draw conclusions about the past, however, reason and observation alone are not sufficient. Events in the past, such as the origins of the earth, are not repeatable. They are history. Therefore, they cannot be determined through experimentation. Evidence from the past is inevitably interpreted according to one's presuppositions, and those presuppositions are not based merely on reason but on one's religion. In particular, all the presuppositions of mainstream scientists about origins are arbitrarily anti-theistic."

ATTY PORTER "That is an absurdly broad generalization."

ATTY CARDONA "Not at all. Consider, for example, that evidence in mainstream biology is interpreted by the presupposition that common features in living things imply common descent.[15] The possibility that common features could be the result of common design is arbitrarily rejected, because that would imply a Designer.

"Then consider the presupposition of Charles Lyell, whose three-volume *Principles of Geology* in the 1830s formed the basis of modern geology. Lyell claimed that 'the present is the key to the past,' – that events in the past happened by slow processes over long ages just like the processes we see today. That is the doctrine called uniformitarianism. Why did Lyell come up with this doctrine? Because he was a non-Christian with an expressed distaste for the Flood account in Genesis, saying that we must separate geology from Moses."[16]

ATTY PORTER "Well, as Judge Jones ruled, natural phenomena should be explained by natural causes. A Flood narrative is surely not needed."

ATTY CARDONA "Lyell's uniformitarianism has not fared well, however. Non-Christian geologist Derek Ager observed in 1993 that Lyell's doctrine had been 'brainwashing' geologists into making erroneous conclusions.[17] Ager had a different presupposition; namely that many geological formations can be explained by various catastrophes separated by long ages.[18] Even before Lyell, non-Christian geologist Georges Cuvier operated with the same presupposition as Ager's."

ATTY PORTER "That is just another example of how science is self-correcting."

ATTY CARDONA "Religion is surely not self-correcting, since competing religions have continued to exist for millennia. To the extent that theories about origins are based on inherently religious presuppositions, we should not expect a resolution of their conflicting conclusions."

ATTY PORTER "How about the Big Bang? Surely no one anymore believes the old idea that the universe had no beginning."

ATTY CARDONA "The Big Bang has its own presupposition. It is used to find solutions of Einstein's equations of general relativity. It is called the cosmological or Copernican principle. Astronomer Edwin Hubble acknowledged that it is just a 'sheer assumption.' He described the presupposition this way: 'There must be no favoured location in the universe, no centre, no boundary, all must see the universe alike.' Later Stephen Hawking and others acknowledged that 'we are not able to make cosmological models without some admixture of ideology.'"[19]

ATTY PORTER "What could be controversial or religious about assuming that the universe must appear the same regardless of location? It's totally reasonable."

ATTY CARDONA "It might seem reasonable. Consider, however, this revealing quote from cosmologists Hawking and Ellis:

'In the earliest cosmologies, man placed himself in a commanding position at the center of the universe. Since the time of Copernicus, we have been steadily demoted to a medium sized planet going round a medium sized star on the outer edge of a fairly average galaxy, which is itself one of a local group of galaxies. Indeed, we are not so democratic that we would not claim our position in space is specially distinguished in any way. We shall, following Bondi, call this assumption the *Copernican principle*.'[20]

"Notice first of all, the admission that there is a fundamental *assumption*, which stems from an *ideology*. This is not something that stems from reason alone. As observed by physicist Dr. Russell Humphreys:

"'…the Bible is quite clear about the centrality of our planet in God's plans. Genesis mentions the earth on the first day and third day, well before God made the sun, moon, and stars on the fourth day. It was a sin on this planet that subjected the whole universe to groaning and travailing. It was to this planet that the Creator came to die on the cross and deliver not only us, but also the entire physical cosmos from the consequences of that first sin. God's eternal throne will be on earth… To escape consciousness of the scrutiny of such a God, secularists have worked hard to belittle our location and us.'[21]

"Dr. Humphreys himself examined the consequences of using a different presupposition in Einstein's equations. By assuming that the universe is bounded and does have a center, he derived solutions of those equations consistent with the Biblical account of a young earth.

"In conclusion, I submit that Judge Jones' ruling should not be considered binding by this court. I have demonstrated that religion is pervasive in all considerations of origins. Denying consideration of Genesis in such a context gives preference to another religion, pantheism in particular. No school board should be demanding such a preference."

JUDGE JACOBSEN "The court is adjourned until tomorrow morning."

THE COURTROOM HALLWAY

Jason and his attorney, Brian, walked out of the courtroom and began to review the afternoon's arguments while walking down the hallway.

"Jason, do you remember the fuel truck blown up by the South Sudanese? I hope I have similarly destroyed the common claim that science must be separated from the Bible," Brian said.

He stopped and motioned for Jason to grab a bench in the hallway. "And just as religion motivated the soldiers on *both* sides, I've attempted to show how religion motivates *both sides* in this debate. We need to dismantle the notion that this is a case of science versus religion."

Jason smiled impishly and said, "I guess we know what the 'P' in Mr. Porter's name stands for. He's an advocate for pantheism."

Brian concluded, "Let's just pray for Attorney Porter and for a favorable ruling in the morning."

Jason added, "We should also pray for our first expert witnesses, that they'll be ready tomorrow. Speaking of witnesses, I wonder if we have enough funds, as of now, to pay for the travel expenses of our expert witnesses." Jason worried again about his legal fund.

"There's some time yet before the bills have to be paid," Brian replied.

MONDAY EVENING

THE RADCLIFFE FAMILY APARTMENT

Jason and Carol got supper ready and set the kitchen table before calling up to Collin in his room who was enthralled in his favorite dinosaur book. After a second and louder call, Collin bounded down the stairs ready to eat.

As they took their seats Jason began singing and they all joined in: "The Lord is good, His mercy everlasting, and the truth of the Lord endures forever." Collin wolfed down his dinner and was about to get up from the table when Jason said, "Let's have a short Bible time first." So he read Psalm 100 (the origin of their song) and they prayed about the trial.

"Are you going to win, Daddy?" asked Collin. "My friend Brad at school keeps asking me."

"It's in God's hands, Collin" Jason replied.

After supper, Jason asked Carol, "Were they able to get a substitute teacher to cover for you tomorrow?"

"Yes, but the principal told me she thought you should drop the court case and agree to take your extra books out of the classroom."

"Hmm, I hope that Clark Elementary doesn't get any ideas about firing you, too. You've shared a little of your faith there also."

"What I'm worried about is Brian's legal fees. We're doing okay for now on my salary, but your attorney is going to cost us a bunch. And we were going to save some of your salary so we could make a down payment on a home."

Jason reminded Carol about the crowdfunding they'd set up for the legal fees. Nonetheless, Carol could not help expressing her concern. "Yes, but it's running way behind our expected expenses."

"Let's not worry now and be thankful that our church friend, Brandon Taylor, told us about Brian Cardona. They were classmates at Branchburg High School years ago and have kept in touch ever since."

TUESDAY MORNING

THE COURTHOUSE CAFETERIA

Jason and Brian met up for a light breakfast at the courthouse cafeteria before the trial resumed. Over coffee and a croissant, Jason scrolled through his favorite news site on his phone. He quickly noticed the clickbait headline, "Evangelical Hate at Branchburg School Trial." The first line read, "Evangelical hate raised its ugly head again in the Branchburg school trial yesterday as attorney, Brian Cardona, tried to paint scientists as pantheists."

"Brian, why would this reporter bring up that old canard about how evangelicalism is founded on hatred? I thought Henry Manning was a respected reporter. We're even praying for Attorney Porter, just as Jesus taught us to pray for our enemies."

Brian thought for a while and remarked, "Well, Manning doesn't know about our prayers. In the circle of his peers, he surely doesn't know much about evangelicals either. Maybe he was turned off once by some overly emotional preacher. We'll just have to pray for him too.

"And most people have never understood our insight about how this conflict is fundamentally a religious one. Our religion shapes how we look at everything. As Jesus Himself observed, 'The lamp of the body is the eye. If therefore your eye is good, your whole body will be full of light. But if your eye is bad, your whole body will be full of darkness.'[22] We'd better get going, however. The trial's set to start in fifteen minutes. I hope the judge agrees with our argument from yesterday. Otherwise, our case will be dismissed."

TUESDAY MORNING

THE COURTROOM

PRE-TRIAL MOTIONS

Is Creation Science Admissible Evidence?

JUDGE JACOBSEN "Good morning. The court is in session. The court finds with the plaintiff that questions concerning origins are inherently religious in nature. Therefore, the defendant's motion to dismiss this case is denied. Before we proceed with the opening statements by the attorneys, however, there seems to be more pretrial business to deal with. Mr. Porter, I understand that you have some concerns about the presentation of evidence in this case."

ATTY PORTER "Yes, your honor. I understand that plaintiff's counsel is planning to present evidence from so-called creationists. I respectfully submit that there are grounds why such evidence is inadmissible in this court."

JUDGE JACOBSEN "What reasons are you referring to?"

ATTY PORTER "Allow me to cite three common criteria for admitting evidence in a trial. To be admissible, evidence must be testable, peer reviewed, and generally accepted by scientists. I submit that creationist evidence fails to satisfy any of these criteria and therefore should not be admissible in this court."

JUDGE JACOBSEN "Mr. Cardona, do you envision that this will be an extensive discussion?"

ATTY CARDONA "It might be, since my opponent is making claims that are very common and pervasive."

JUDGE JACOBSEN "Then if there is no objection, let me allow the witnesses here present to retire from this courtroom until this afternoon at 1:30."

ATTY CARDONA "No objection."

ATTY PORTER "No objection."

JUDGE JACOBSEN "All right, Mr. Porter, please support your claims."

ATTY PORTER "Firstly, plaintiff's creationist evidence is not testable. Rather, it is speculation and myth."

ATTY CARDONA "Evidence about origins is not subject to experimentation because the events cannot be repeated. Nevertheless, interpretations of the evidence can be checked or tested by observations. I am prepared to provide witnesses representing creation scientists who *have* made testable theories. Later observations confirmed predictions made from those theories. Those theories involved radioactive decay, the magnetic fields of the planets, coal formation and mitochondrial DNA. In contrast, evolutionists have not produced testable theories. They simply use evolutionary theories to try and explain whatever they find."

ATTY PORTER "It is false to claim that evolution is not testable. For example, evolutionists have observed evolution in action in the case of sickle cell anemia, acquired resistance of diseases to antibiotics, and appearance of new species such as in the class of the finches that Darwin observed."

ATTY CARDONA "All of these examples you mention only show minor changes. They do not demonstrate the development of new organisms with new information. In particular, some mutations involving a loss of information and overall loss of viability can produce localized advantages. Such is the case with sickle cell anemia which provides resistance against malaria, and other changes in microbes that provide resistance to specific antibiotics. In addition, once the environment is changed back to its original state, variations in birds or peppered moths, for example, often are reversed. In no case is a new kind of animal observed. Similarly, breeding of animals has its limits. Cats are always cats and dogs are always dogs, even if new species are produced. I am prepared to provide witnesses representing creation scientists who recently have shown how features built into DNA allow species to adapt to their environment without mutations."

Atty Porter "All these obstacles can be overcome given enough time, such as the millions of years over which evolution occurred. If creationists' evidence were testable, it would be supported by grants from respectable institutions such as the National Institutes of Health (NIH). NIH currently supports research at numerous university departments of evolutionary biology. On the contrary, creationists' work has not even been peer reviewed in standard journals."

- - -

Just then, Jason noticed his wife and son walking into the courtroom and ready to take a seat. He quickly got up and walked down the side aisle, motioning for them all to leave the courtroom.

Outside the courtroom Jason told Carol, "Attorney Porter brought up another objection, so the formal trial won't start 'til this afternoon. Can you and Collin come back by 2? The opening statements should be over by then."

"But I want to hear everything," Collin interjected.

"Okay," Carol replied, "I'll just take Collin over to the Cheshire Cat Bookstore and then we'll have some lunch at the Hamburger Garden next door."

"I'll join you there if there's enough time," said Jason. Jason and Carol exchanged a quick kiss, and Jason quietly reentered the courtroom.

- - -

ATTY CARDONA "Creation scientists do, in fact, publish many excellent papers in peer-reviewed journals such as the *Creation Research Society Quarterly*, *Answers Research Journal*, and *Journal of Creation*."

ATTY PORTER "Those are all creationist journals, not standard scientific journals."

ATTY CARDONA "Creation scientists occasionally do have their papers accepted in mainstream scientific journals, especially if their identity as creation scientists is not known. However, most of the time their papers are arbitrarily rejected as non-scientific when their identity is known.[23] Hence they are forced to publish their work in creation science journals.

"The history of science contains many instances where the proponent of a new paradigm was initially ridiculed, such as Ignaz Semmelweis in medicine, Alfred Wegener in geophysics and J Harlan Bretz in geology. Semmelweis dramatically reduced maternal mortality by requiring that physicians wash their hands in a chlorine solution before delivering babies. Nevertheless, published medical works either ignored or suppressed his teachings for many years. Similarly, geologists ignored or suppressed for many years the theory of plate tectonics developed by Alfred Wegener and the theory of catastrophic formation of the Scablands in Washington State developed by J. Harlan Bretz. It is no wonder that creation scientists are treated similarly."

ATTY PORTER "Let us just remember that the Scopes Trial, already one hundred years ago, demonstrated the bankruptcy of fundamentalist theories."

ATTY CARDONA "On the contrary, we should remember the evidence that was common at the time of the Scopes Trial in support of human evolution. This evidence included the so-called transitional forms called Piltdown Man and Nebraska Man. After more than 30 years, during which time many Ph.D. theses were written about Piltdown Man, a rather simple investigation finally showed that Piltdown Man was a crude hoax. Investigations after the Scopes Trial also showed that Nebraska Man was a fantasy based on a single pig's tooth. Similarly, other evidence for evolution presented in newspaper reports of the Scopes Trail has since been discredited.[24]

"It is also not generally realized that many who were called 'fundamentalists' a hundred years ago favored an old-earth reading of Genesis 1, not the plain reading. For example, R. A. Torrey wrote some of the booklets called *The Fundamentals*. He was one of the founders of the Bible Institute of Los Angeles, now Biola University, but had studied under old-earth geologist James Dwight Dana while at Yale. Similarly, J. Gresham Machen, at the center of the Fundamentalist-Modernist controversy at Princeton Theological Seminary in the 1920s, held old-earth views.[25]

"Even William Jennings Bryan, who argued against human evolution at the Scopes Trial, would not affirm that the days in Genesis 1 were 24-hour days. The evidence we wish to present in this trial is from scientists who do believe in a young earth, since my client has had their material in his classroom."

ATTY PORTER "So that means your client is even more extreme than the fundamentalists?"

ATTY CARDONA "Fundamentalists a hundred years ago were influenced by old-earth ideas that were prevalent in academia. They generally did not realize the pantheistic presuppositions behind those ideas. They also, of course, were not aware of the excellent work of creation scientists presented in the past fifty years or so. That work is extreme only in the sense of being extremely thorough, well substantiated and, in several cases, verified by fulfilled predictions."

ATTY PORTER "Whatever the situation of infighting may be among fundamentalists, creationists' work is not generally accepted by scientists. Accordingly, the Branchburg school district has claimed correctly that creationism is a fringe theory not generally accepted by scientists and therefore should not be taught in school.

"Even many people who call themselves Christians today do not believe that the Genesis account is a reliable description of physical origins. For example, Christian apologetics author William Lane Craig states that 'young earth creationism's scientific claim is wildly implausible' in his recent book *In Quest of the Historical Adam*.[26] Oxford mathematics professor John Lennox, a well-known Christian apologist, wrote about 'the current scientific evidence for an ancient earth,' and concluded 'we would be very unwise to ignore science through obscurantism or fear, and present to the world an image of Christianity that is anti-intellectual.'[27] And Francis Collins, former director of the National Institutes of Health and author of *The Language of God: A Scientist Presents Evidence for Belief*, characterized a literal view of Genesis 1 and 2 as 'a very narrow perspective that will put our faith at risk of looking ridiculous.'[28]

"In conclusion, your honor, let me just cite Christian professor of history Mark Noll. In the Afterword of the 2022 printing of *The Scandal of the Evangelical Mind* he wrote, 'Visitors by the tens of thousands come every year for enlightenment on these questions to Ark Encounter, "a Christian religious and creationist theme park" in Kentucky. Its picture of early human history has no standing among formally credentialed scientists.'[29] I have shown that creationist evidence is not testable, not peer-reviewed, and not generally accepted."

ATTY CARDONA "Noll wrote in his book that he had studied the rise of the modern creationist movement. If he had really done his homework, he could easily have found the creationist website, www.creation.com for example, and seen a partial list with over 100 Ph.D. scientists who hold a young-earth view. Of course, the relative number of adherents doesn't necessarily indicate the truth of an idea, as I have already mentioned in the cases of Semmelweis, Wegener and Bretz. Your honor, I have refuted the claims of the defense, so in all fairness the evidence we wish to present should be permitted."

JUDGE JACOBSEN "The court is adjourned until this afternoon."

THE COURTROOM HALLWAY

In regular fashion, Jason and Brian discussed the morning's proceedings as they walked out of the courtroom and down the hallway.

Brian remarked, "Remember the South Sudanese again? Yesterday we destroyed the fuel truck that represented the claim that science must be separated from the Bible. We also exposed the religion behind that claim, just like the religion behind the Northern Sudanese soldiers. Today I had to deal with the ammunition truck, namely, the claim that no serious scientists believe that the earth is young. Thankfully, I think this morning's proceedings went okay. I hope the judge agrees."

Jason tried to encourage Brian, saying, "I think you did great." He thought for a minute and added, "You know, it's ironic that Attorney Porter is trying to keep creation science out of this trial. Remember the Scopes Trial? After some testimony for evolution by one expert witness, the prosecution in that trial argued that such testimony was not relevant, and the judge concurred. The judge only allowed further testimony by expert witnesses to be inserted into the record as written affidavits."

Brian responded, "While I was studying up for this trial, I also read about a comment about that from the legislator who actually wrote the Tennessee law prohibiting the teaching of human evolution in schools. That was the law used by the prosecution against John Scopes. The legislator, John Butler, indicated he regretted that scientific evidence from expert witnesses on either side was not allowed as testimony in the court."[30, 31]

Changing the subject, Brian added, "It was a shame that your wife and son came for nothing this morning, but trials often take unexpected turns."

"No problem," Jason said. "They got to spend some time in the Cheshire Cat Bookstore. I think there's enough time to join them for lunch at the hamburger place next door. See you at 1:30."

"Don't be late," Brian added.

TUESDAY NOON

THE HAMBURGER GARDEN

"What book did you get?" Jason asked Collin as they sat down with their hamburgers.

"It's called *Drake and the Dragons*," Collin announced.

"What's it about?"

"There's this kid, Drake, who goes exploring and finds real rock carvings that look like dragons, including one that's breathing fire. Look here – this one really looks like an allosaur dinosaur."

"Yeah, I see that! The book of Job in the Bible describes a fire-breathing sea creature, too."[32]

"Do you think people might really have seen those?" Collin asked with intense curiosity.

"If they could draw them, they certainly could have seen them, don't you think?" Jason enjoyed watching Collin's eyes widen.

Turning to Carol, Jason asked, "Is that all you're eating?"

"Yes, love, the garden salad is about all I can handle. I'm too anxious about this afternoon to eat anything else," Carol sighed.

"Well," Jason perked up, "I'm quite confident the judge will let the trial move forward. He just has to toss out the monkey wrench Attorney Porter tried to throw in today."

TUESDAY AFTERNOON

THE COURTROOM

As Jason and Brian chatted, they noticed the judge walking into the courtroom. The judge seemed to recognize a man preparing to write some notes in the back of the room, but evidently he was not so sure, so he asked, "Who are you?"

The man quickly stood up. "I'm Henry Manning of the Branchburg Times, your honor."

Another man also stood up, whom the judge didn't recognize. "And who are you?" asked Judge Jacobsen.

"Douglas Thomason of the Dale County News-Register, your honor." The judge then proceeded to his bench at the front and sat down.

THE TRIAL BEGINS

Opening Statements

JUDGE JACOBSEN "The court is in session. It is the finding of this court that the defendant did not demonstrate convincingly that plaintiff's evidence from certain expert witnesses should be excluded. So the attorneys may now proceed with their opening statements. Are you ready, Mr. Cardona?"

ATTY CARDONA "Yes."

JUDGE JACOBSEN "Please proceed."

ATTY CARDONA "I intend to show in this trial, your honor, that my client, Mr. Jason Radcliffe, has been wrongfully and illegally terminated from his position as science teacher at Branchburg High School. The defendant, the Branchburg school board, claims that their action was justified due to certain books my client placed in his classroom library. The defendant claims that these books were propagating creationist religion and were therefore inappropriate in a science classroom. I will show that my client did not coerce any students to read or believe the material in these books. Therefore, he was free to express his religion by making them available.

"I will also show that anti-theistic religion is typically behind the presuppositions of science books promoting opposite views of origins. A candid acknowledgment of this situation was provided by the late Harvard geneticist Richard Lewontin, who wrote, and I quote:

"'Our willingness to accept scientific claims that are against common sense is the key to an understanding of the real struggle between science and the supernatural. We take the side of science *in spite* of the patent absurdity of some of its constructs, *in spite* of its failure to fulfill many of its extravagant promises of health and life, *in spite* of the tolerance of the scientific community for unsubstantiated just-so stories, because we have a prior commitment, a commitment to materialism. It is not that the methods and institutions of science somehow compel us to accept a material explanation of the phenomenal world, but, on the contrary, that we are forced by our *a priori* adherence to material causes to create an apparatus of investigation and a set of concepts that produce material explanations, no matter how counter-intuitive, no matter how mystifying to the uninitiated. Moreover, that materialism is absolute, for we cannot allow a Divine Foot in the door.'[33]

"Materialism, the denial of the supernatural and belief that evolutionary progress is a principle behind Nature, is little more than an expression of a non-theistic religion. It can be identified as a kind of pantheism. Therefore, the science books that my client made available are no more religious than other common books about origins.

"Finally, I will also present expert witnesses who will actually show how creation science explains data concerning origins better than common scientific speculations. One can only conclude then that the defendant needs to reverse its wrongful termination of Jason Radcliffe and reinstate him as science teacher."

JUDGE JACOBSEN "Okay, now, Mr. Porter, you may present your opening statement."

ATTY PORTER "Most of the books inserted by the plaintiff in his classroom library were inspired by the Bible. I will present evidence that one actually presented an openly religious message. Due to its obligation to separate church from state, a public school must be careful not to appear to promote any particular religion.

"I will also present evidence of how the creationist authors of the books in question have attempted to propagate their religion. They do so by injecting the Bible into all sorts of pseudoscience. In addition, I will present evidence from expert witnesses that creationist explanations of natural phenomena have been discredited. On the other hand, our witnesses will show how well-established natural explanations correctly explain natural phenomena. Again, a public school cannot promote any particular religion, such as creationism.

"In summary, the Branchburg school board was certainly correct in terminating the plaintiff's employment."

Judge Jacobsen "All right, let's proceed with the witnesses."

THE PARTIES IN THE CASE

Atty Cardona "I would now like to call on my first witness, Jason Radcliffe. Please tell the court your background, Jason."

Jason Radcliffe "I received a master's degree in physics from the University of Strathburg."

Atty Cardona "What was your most recent employment?"

Jason Radcliffe "A science teacher at Branchburg High School."

Atty Cardona "How long have you taught there?"

Jason Radcliffe "Three years."

Atty Cardona "When did you last work there?"

Jason Radcliffe "Six months ago."

Atty Cardona "That was when you were dismissed, was it not?"

Jason Radcliffe "Yes."

Atty Cardona "What was the reason given to you for your dismissal?"

Jason Radcliffe "The principal said that some books I had placed in my classroom's library were inappropriate."

Atty Cardona "What were some of the titles of the books?"

JASON RADCLIFFE "*The Fossil Record; Earth's Mysterious Magnetism; Thousands…not Billions; Carved in Stone; Genetic Entropy:, Grand Canyon: Monument to an Ancient Earth.*"[34]

ATTY CARDONA "What were the credentials of the authors?"

JASON RADCLIFFE "Except for some authors in the last book I just mentioned, I think they all had Ph.D.s."

ATTY CARDONA "Were they textbooks?"

JASON RADCLIFFE "No."

ATTY CARDONA "How difficult were they to understand?"

JASON RADCLIFFE "They were accessible to general audiences or to students at an advanced high school level. Most of them also had an abundance of photos and diagrams."

ATTY CARDONA "Why did you place these books in the classroom's library?"

JASON RADCLIFFE "They were supplemental books, to help with critical thinking."

ATTY CARDONA "Were all those books by creation scientists?"

JASON RADCLIFFE "All except the last one on the Grand Canyon."

ATTY CARDONA "Why did you include that book?"

JASON RADCLIFFE "I wanted any inquisitive student to be able to compare that book with the others that have a different viewpoint."

ATTY CARDONA "Do the ideas in the books by creation scientists represent your personal viewpoint about origins?"

JASON RADCLIFFE "Yes."

ATTY CARDONA "Do you believe the description of origins in Genesis is literally correct?"

JASON RADCLIFFE "Yes."

ATTY CARDONA "Did you tell your students about these books?"

JASON RADCLIFFE "I mentioned to them that I put some supplemental science books in the library that deal with interpretations about earth's origins. I said they were welcome to borrow any or talk to me after school about them."

ATTY CARDONA "Did you use any of these books in your class lessons?"

JASON RADCLIFFE "No."

ATTY CARDONA "Why not?"

JASON RADCLIFFE "The class lessons only dealt with explanations of repeatable experiments and observations."

ATTY CARDONA "Did other teachers in your school have libraries in their classrooms?"

JASON RADCLIFFE "I understood that it was a fairly common practice."

ATTY CARDONA "Were you ever told that such classroom libraries were not allowed in your school?"

JASON RADCLIFFE "Never."

ATTY CARDONA "Did any of your students talk to you about the books or ask if they could borrow one?"

JASON RADCLIFFE "Yes, there were two."

ATTY CARDONA "What were their names?"

JASON RADCLIFFE "Peter Benson and Stuart Donner."

ATTY CARDONA "What books did they borrow?"

JASON RADCLIFFE "Peter Benson took the books on geology: *Carved in Stone* and *Grand Canyon: Monument to an Ancient Earth.* Stuart Donner took the book on *Earth's Mysterious Magnetism.*"

ATTY CARDONA "Did either of them talk to you about the books?"

Jason Radcliffe "Peter thanked me for letting him borrow them."

Atty Cardona "Did Stuart say anything to you about the one he borrowed?"

Jason Radcliffe "No."

Atty Cardona "No further questions. Your witness, Mr. Porter."

Atty Porter "Mr. Radcliffe, are you aware that creationist material is religious?"

Jason Radcliffe "It bases its interpretations on religious presuppositions, yes."

Atty Porter "What are those presuppositions?"

Jason Radcliffe "That there is a Creator God, that He has revealed events about our origins in the Bible, and that we were made in His image so that we can understand His creation."

Atty Porter "What point is there to have religious books in a science classroom?"

Jason Radcliffe "All science books dealing with origins and nonrepeatable events in the past are based on some religious presuppositions."

Atty Porter "What are the presuppositions you are claiming for common science books about our origins?"

Jason Radcliffe "Conclusions in science books dealing with origins commonly derive from materialist or naturalist assumptions."

Atty Porter "What is religious about that?"

Jason Radcliffe "Denying the supernatural and assuming that evolutionary progress is a principle of nature is an expression of a non-theistic religion like pantheism."

ATTY PORTER "No further questions for Jason. If Mr. Cardona has no more witnesses, I would like to call my witness, Dr. Jackie Kennard."

ATTY CARDONA "I have no more witnesses to call at this point."

ATTY PORTER "Dr. Kennard, please tell us your background."

DR. KENNARD "I have a Master's degree and Ph.D. in education from the University of Strathburg."

ATTY PORTER "You are an employee of Branchburg High School, correct?"

DR. KENNARD "Yes."

ATTY PORTER "What is your position there?"

DR. KENNARD "I am the principal."

ATTY PORTER "And Jason Radcliffe was a science teacher at your school, correct?"

DR. KENNARD "Yes."

ATTY PORTER "How did you learn about the books in the library of Mr. Radcliffe's classroom?"

DR. KENNARD "A student showed me one of the books."

ATTY PORTER "What was the student's name?"

DR. KENNARD "Stuart Donner."

ATTY PORTER "And what was the title of the book?"

DR. KENNARD "I believe it was something about the earth's magnetism."

ATTY PORTER "Did Stuart Donner say anything to you about the book?"

DR. KENNARD "Yes, he was offended that at the end of the book there was a picture of a cross and a claim that we are accountable to Jesus and God."

ATTY PORTER "Were you concerned about that?"

DR. KENNARD "Yes."

ATTY PORTER "Why was that?"

DR. KENNARD "The book was propagating religion, which has no place in a science classroom."

ATTY PORTER "Was there any other reason for your concern?"

DR. KENNARD "Yes. Books like that will confuse students and likely will disincline them to pursue any career in science."

ATTY PORTER "What did you do when you found out about these books?"

DR. KENNARD "I informed Mr. Radcliffe about my concerns and requested that he remove the books from his classroom."

ATTY PORTER "Did he comply with your request?"

DR. KENNARD "No."

ATTY PORTER "Did he tell you why?"

DR. KENNARD "He said something about not forcing anything on his students."

ATTY PORTER "What did you do then?"

DR. KENNARD "I informed the school board and recommended that they dismiss the teacher from his position."

ATTY PORTER "No further questions. Your witness, Mr. Cardona."

ATTY CARDONA "Dr. Kennard, science teacher Radcliffe has been teaching at your school for three years, correct?"

DR. KENNARD "Yes."

ATTY CARDONA "Has his performance been acceptable?"

DR. KENNARD "He has been given good ratings overall."

ATTY CARDONA "Did any student complain about Mr. Radcliffe prior to the complaint from Stuart Donner about the book on the earth's magnetism?"

Dr. Kennard "No."

Atty Cardona "No further questions."

Judge Jacobsen "I understand that counsel will next call several scientists as expert witnesses. Since we have covered enough ground this afternoon, the court is adjourned again until tomorrow morning. Counsel, please make sure you and your witnesses are on time."

TUESDAY EVENING

THE RADCLIFFE FAMILY APARTMENT

"Daddy, you were great today! So was Mr. Cardona." Collin jumped in the air after walking in the door with his mom and dad.

"Thank you, Collin. I'm happy to see how polite you were to the others, too." Jason leaned over and looked Collin in the eye and gave him a fist bump. "Right now, though, I feel like I'd better go rest for a few minutes. Deal?"

"Deal, daddy!"

"No worries," Carol said, "I'll cook up some spaghetti and meatballs I have in the freezer."

"Too bad it's not spring break and you had to take a day off." Jason remarked. "Easter week came a bit too late for that this year."

"It was a good day, and worth it," Carol declared.

"Before I forget to tell you, Collin," Jason remarked, "Brad's mom – you know, the one we carpool with – is going to take you both ways for school the rest of this week."

"Okay," Collin said, "she's nice."

WEDNESDAY MORNING

THE COURTHOUSE CAFETERIA

The next morning, Jason and Brian met up again at the cafeteria before the trial resumed. This time, Jason didn't waste any time looking for Henry Manning's reporting on the previous day's trial proceedings. Jason scrolled through his phone and was surprised, instead, to find an article by a reporter named Douglas Thomason with the headline, "Teacher's Attorney More Radical Than the Fundamentalists."

"Look at this, Brian, how did Thomason get that idea?" Jason wondered.

"Remember yesterday when I mentioned that many fundamentalists a hundred years ago accepted that the earth is very old, but that we wish to present evidence consistent with a plain young earth reading of Genesis? In the world's eyes, that would make us even more extreme and reactionary, if you will, than fundamentalists. Since they already think that fundamentalists are a fringe group, we must be even more crazy. I hope the judge doesn't think like Thomason. Let's go now so we can be early and make sure our witnesses are all there and ready."

WEDNESDAY MORNING

THE COURTROOM

JUDGE JACOBSEN "The court is again in session. Mr. Cardona, I understand that you wish to present evidence for your claim that a plain reading of Genesis is a reliable description of the world's physical origins."

ATTY CARDONA "Yes, your honor, I have witnesses in three areas: biology, geology, and cosmology. In each of these areas, there are subtopics."

JUDGE JACOBSEN "Please separate your case by subtopic. You may present your witness or witnesses and the defendant's attorney may cross-examine them. While in the same subtopic, the defendant's attorney may then present his own witness or witnesses and you may cross-examine them. In that way, we can focus on all the relevant witnesses before moving on to the next topic."

ATTY CARDONA "Thank you. I would like to begin with evidence from biology, in particular evidence about the origin of life."

BIOLOGY

Origin of Life

ATTY CARDONA "For my first witness, I would like to call Witness 1, representing the work of Louis Pasteur, a 19th century French chemist. Witness 1, please summarize Pasteur's work for us."

WITNESS 1 "Pasteur was born in 1822 to the family of a poor tanner. He became well-known for his work in the late 1840s demonstrating the rotation of light passing through certain crystals and liquids. After identifying microbes that caused wine and milk to spoil, he invented the remedy that was later called pasteurization in his honor. Later he developed successful vaccines for anthrax and rabies and cures for silkworm diseases."

ATTY CARDONA "What did Pasteur demonstrate that is of most interest to this court?"

WITNESS 1 "Pasteur demonstrated that life only comes from previous life. Other scientists were claiming that meat became rotten, and broth became spoiled by organisms that spontaneously formed from something like a 'life force.' After he had performed several careful experiments, the French Academy of Sciences in 1862 awarded Pasteur the Alhumbert Prize for settling the debate."

ATTY CARDONA "Was Pasteur's result consistent with the account in Genesis 2 that states 'the Lord God formed man of the dust of the ground, and breathed into his nostrils the breath of life, and man became a living being?'"

WITNESS 1 "Yes. The first man surely did not originate spontaneously, but supernaturally."

ATTY CARDONA "No further questions. Your witness, Attorney Porter."

ATTY PORTER "Is there any evidence from Pasteur's notebooks, relatives, and colleagues indicating that he sometimes gave misleading accounts of his discoveries, that he was sometimes unfair and arrogant, that he was a freethinker and that he insisted science should not mix with religion?"

ATTY CARDONA "I object, your honor This is a leading question."

JUDGE JACOBSEN "Objection overruled. Witness 1, you may answer."

WITNESS 1 "I have read about such things, yes."

ATTY PORTER "Based on Pasteur's character and his insistence that science should not mix with religion, I submit that we should not trust his results about spontaneous generation nor their relevance to this court."

ATTY CARDONA "I object. Because he had some character defects, as we all do, does not negate the significance of his experiments. Those experiments stand by themselves, and we may certainly make conclusions from them that affect our religious understanding."

JUDGE JACOBSEN "Objection sustained."

ATTY PORTER "I have no more questions for Witness 1.

ATTY CARDONA "Witness 1, did Pasteur describe his experiments correctly to the French Academy of Sciences?"

WITNESS 1 "Yes. He described them in detail in a series of five lectures to that Academy in 1881."

ATTY CARDONA "Has anyone since then demonstrated spontaneous generation of living organisms?"

WITNESS 1 "No."

ATTY CARDONA "No further questions of Witness 1. I have no more witnesses on this subtopic."

ATTY PORTER "I would like now to introduce expert witness 2, representing the work of Stanley Miller. Witness 2, can you tell us a little bit about his experiments concerning the origin of life?"

WITNESS 2 "In 1953, Dr. Stanley Miller of the University of California at San Diego, reported in the journal *Science* on laboratory experiments of how life could have originated from inorganic (nonliving) matter. The goal was to obtain some amino acids, the building blocks of living things, from an electric discharge in some simple gases. The discharge was to simulate lightning, and the gases were to simulate the original 'primordial soup' of the earth.[35] I submit the following diagram of his experiments."

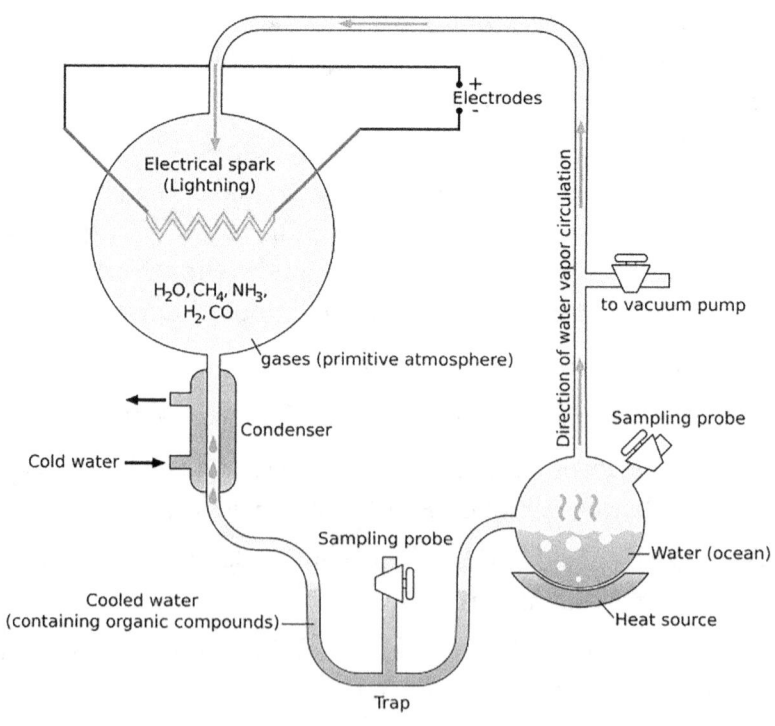

Exhibit 1. *Stanley Miller's Experiment*

Atty Porter "Were the experiments successful in producing amino acids?"

Witness 2 "Yes."

Atty Porter "Are some amino acids like the 'letters' in proteins?"

Witness 2 "Yes."

Atty Porter "Could conditions similar to those in Miller's experiments have resulted in life in the past, even though conditions on the earth at present do not produce life?"

Witness 2 "That seems reasonable. A 'primordial soup' many millions of years ago would not be the same as on our present earth."

Atty Porter "No further questions. Your witness, Attorney Cardona."

Atty Cardona "Is ozone needed in the atmosphere to protect life from being destroyed by ultraviolet radiation from the sun?"

Witness 2 "Yes, at present."

Atty Cardona "Would ozone have been produced from oxygen by the sparks in Miller's experiments?"

Witness 2 "Yes."

Atty Cardona "Was there any oxygen present in the flasks in Miller's experiments?"

Witness 2 "No."

Atty Cardona "Why is that?"

Witness 2 "Oxygen would have destroyed amino acids that were produced."

Atty Cardona "How then was Miller's version of the 'primordial soup' relevant to the formation of life?"

Witness 2 "Maybe oxygen came into the atmosphere later after life had already been formed."

Atty Cardona "I notice a 'trap' in the diagram of the experimental apparatus that you presented. What was the function of that trap?"

Witness 2 "The trap isolated the amino acids that were formed."

Atty Cardona "Is it true that without the trap, any amino acids would have disintegrated as soon as they were formed back into the original gases in the 'soup?'"

Witness 2 "Yes."

Atty Cardona "Why is that?"

Witness 2 "Because chemical equilibrium favors the simple gases."

Atty Cardona "How could there have been such a 'trap' in the primordial soup?"

Witness 2 "That would be natural selection."

Atty Cardona "What would be the mechanism for such 'natural selection?'"

Witness 2 "We don't know the details at present. I understand that another witness will speak about natural selection."

Atty Cardona "What is the difference between left-handed and right-handed amino acids?"

Witness 2 "Left-handed amino acids rotate light passing through them counterclockwise while right-handed amino acids rotate light clockwise. The situation is the same in some crystals and solutions that Pasteur studied."

Atty Cardona "What forms of amino acids were found in the trap in Miller's experiments?"

Witness 2 "Both left-handed and right-handed amino acids."

Atty Cardona "Is it true that almost all living things only contain left-handed amino acids?"

Witness 2 "Yes."

ATTY CARDONA "How then could Miller's experiment be relevant to the origin of life?"

WITNESS 2 "Perhaps the fraction of sunlight that is circularly polarized could have destroyed the right-handed amino acids, or maybe a high magnetic field at the earth's surface could cause left-handed amino acids to accumulate preferentially. Many possibilities have been suggested."

ATTY CARDONA "Those possibilities are all very speculative, correct?"

WITNESS 2 "At present, yes"

ATTY CARDONA "No further questions of Witness 2."

JUDGE JACOBSEN "Attorney Porter, do you have any further witnesses on this subtopic?"

ATTY PORTER "No."

JUDGE JACOBSEN "Then let's take a short break. Please be back in 15 minutes."

THE COURTROOM HALLWAY

As Jason and Brian walk out of the courtroom, Brian remarked, "Did you ever read the verse in Proverbs that says, 'The first one to plead his cause seems right, until his neighbor comes and examines him?'[36] That is just what we're doing."

"Yeah, that's really important. But how did you know what questions to ask the last witness?"

"Well," Brian replied, "before trial, attorneys are given a list of the witnesses that may be called by the other side. Then we have to do our homework."

Jason observed, "You know, there is a really outstanding scientist named Dr. James Tour at Rice University. He's working on this very issue of the origin of life. He's a Christian who recently challenged many scientists who believe life came about by chance to debate him. Only one responded. In the debate, Dr. Tour pointed out that scientists keep discovering how cells are much more complicated than previously thought. So the task of his opponents keeps getting harder. His opponent responded with a little Lego model."[37]

"Legos can be really complicated and impressive," Brian quipped.

"Yeah, right," Jason responded. "Try to make one that reproduces itself, then."

"Okay, you win. I've got to concentrate on the next witnesses rather than debating you."

THE COURTROOM

Everyone resumed their seats in the courtroom and Judge Jacobsen called the court back in session.

BIOLOGY

Natural Selection

ATTY CARDONA "Now let's move onto the next subtopic of natural selection."

ATTY PORTER "The idea of natural selection is commonly associated with Charles Darwin. Attorney Cardona, would you therefore allow me to present my witness first in this subtopic?"

ATTY CARDONA "Yes, if that is acceptable to this court."

JUDGE JACOBSEN "You may proceed, Mr. Porter."

ATTY PORTER "Let me now call Witness 3, representing the views of Charles Darwin. Witness 3, please review for us the life of Darwin."

WITNESS 3 "Charles Darwin was born in 1809 as the son of a wealthy doctor in England. His grandfather, Erasmus Darwin, had written the poetic book *Zoonomia* that described gradual evolution and descent of life from a common ancestor. After Charles disliked the study of medicine at Edinburgh University, his father sent him to Cambridge University in 1828 to prepare for life as a parson. While there, Charles met parsons who were also naturalists, and Charles liked the works of William Paley, including *Evidences of Christianity* and *Natural Theology*. Darwin also encountered the work of Jean-Baptiste Lamarck, who had proposed a theory of biological evolution.

"From 1831 to 1836 he traveled around the world on the *HMS Beagle*, taking many notes on what he saw. In particular, he studied variations in bird species on the Galapagos Islands. When he returned home, he became acquainted with Charles Lyell, whose first volume of *Principles of Geology* he had taken on the *Beagle*. Darwin had used Lyell's theories about slow geological changes over long ages to interpret his observations on that voyage. He worked with anatomist Richard Owen to study the fossil bone specimens he brought back, and he also worked with zoologists to study his plant and animal specimens.

"He studied the selective breeding done by farmers along with ideas of Malthus on overpopulation. He also slowly developed his ideas of natural selection as the way that overpopulation was prevented in nature. He published the first edition of *On the Origin of Species* in 1859. Then in 1871 his theory of human evolution in *The Descent of Man*."

ATTY PORTER "What was particularly new about *On the Origin of Species*?"

WITNESS 3 "It showed that species can change into new species, that natural selection provides the means for that change, and that fossils show the record of those changes."

ATTY PORTER "What did Darwin's book show from the fossil record?"

WITNESS 3 "Darwin showed evidence from the fossils that simple living things evolved into more complex living things, the simpler ones being lower in the geological column and therefore older."

ATTY PORTER "Why was the idea that species could change something new?"

WITNESS 3 "Before Darwin's book was published, it was generally supposed that the Genesis account in the Bible implied fixity of species."

ATTY PORTER "Where does the Bible say that?"

WITNESS 3 "Genesis 1, verses 12, 21, and 24 state that God made trees, herbs, sea creatures, birds, cattle, creeping things and beasts of the earth each according to their kind."

ATTY PORTER "No further questions at this time. Your witness, Attorney Cardona."

ATTY CARDONA "Please remind us, what are the generally accepted classifications of animals above the level of species?"

WITNESS 3 "The next level above species is genus, and above that is family."

ATTY CARDONA "So in a family there can be many genera, and in a genus there can be many species, correct?"

WITNESS 3 "Correct."

ATTY CARDONA "Is it not true that scholars before Darwin generally used the term 'species' interchangeably with the term 'kind' in Genesis, such as the dog kind and the cat kind?"

WITNESS 3 "That is true."

ATTY CARDONA "Would it not be fair to conclude that what Genesis means by 'kind' is often roughly equivalent to 'family?'"

WITNESS 3 "Some people claim that."

ATTY CARDONA "Is it fair to say that Darwin was impressed by the variety of animals breeders could produce?"

WITNESS 3 "Yes."

ATTY CARDONA "Did Darwin ever observe a dog being bred into a cat or a cat into a dog?"

WITNESS 3 "No. That would be impossible."

ATTY CARDONA "Why is that?"

WITNESS 3 "Dogs and cats are genetically incompatible."

ATTY CARDONA "Is it reasonable to say then that the dog kind and the cat kind are fixed, but that the various species within the dog kind are not fixed?"

WITNESS 3 "That would be reasonable."

ATTY CARDONA "So the Genesis account doesn't really imply fixity of species, only fixity of kinds, is that correct?"

WITNESS 3 "I suppose that is correct."

ATTY CARDONA "Darwin assumed that cats and dogs had a common ancestor, correct?"

WITNESS 3 "I don't remember that he explicitly said that."

ATTY CARDONA "But he assumed that all life began with a single common ancestor, correct?"

WITNESS 3 "Yes."

ATTY CARDONA "How did he know that?"

WITNESS 3 "It was just logical."

ATTY CARDONA "Is it not just as logical to believe that life was created in separate kinds as described in Genesis chapter one?"

WITNESS 3 "Scientists don't believe that."

ATTY CARDONA "But nonetheless is it logical?"

WITNESS 3 "I don't think so."

ATTY CARDONA "Why not?"

WITNESS 3 "I'd have to think about it."

ATTY CARDONA "Did Darwin explain how the single common ancestor of life came into existence?"

WITNESS 3 "No."

ATTY CARDONA "Is it not true he just assumed it was there for natural selection to work on?"

WITNESS 3 "That is true."

ATTY CARDONA "Did Darwin demonstrate a genetic mechanism for how natural selection could produce new organisms, such as dogs and cats, from the same ancestor?"

WITNESS 3 "No. Darwin did not know genetics. But we now know that natural selection acting on random genetic mutations can be the process for evolution."

ATTY CARDONA "That is called the Modern Synthesis, correct?"

WITNESS 3 "Correct."

ATTY CARDONA "Are you familiar with the invitation-only symposium held at Altenberg, Austria, in July 2008, attended by 16 evolutionary scientists, called the Altenberg 16?"

WITNESS 3 "Yes."

ATTY CARDONA "I submit to you this quote from a reporter who attended that symposium: 'While the Altenberg 16 have roots in neo-Darwinian theory, they recognize the need to challenge the prevailing Modern Synthesis, *because there's too much it doesn't explain* [emphasis added].[38] Would you consider that a fair assessment?"

WITNESS 3 "All science must continually be open to refinement as new data are discovered."

ATTY CARDONA "What did Darwin say was the weakest feature of his theory?"

ATTY PORTER "Objection, your honor."

JUDGE JACOBSEN "Objection sustained. You do not have to answer that question, Witness 3."

ATTY CARDONA "Did Darwin write that the paucity of transitional forms in the fossil record was the most obvious and gravest objection to his theory?"

WITNESS 3 "Yes."

ATTY CARDONA "How did Darwin envision that this objection would be resolved?"

WITNESS 3 "Darwin supposed that fossil exploration was only in its infancy in his day, but that over time many more transitional forms would be discovered."

ATTY CARDONA "What examples are there then of true transitional forms that have been discovered since Darwin?"

WITNESS 3 "Well, there is *Archeopteryx* representing a transition from reptile to bird, *Tiktaalik* representing a transition from fish to amphibian, and *Australopithecus*, representing a transition from ape to man."

ATTY CARDONA "What were the features of *Archeopteryx* that are like those of reptiles?"

WITNESS 3 "It had teeth, claws on its wing, and a tail."

ATTY CARDONA "What were its features that were like a bird?"

WITNESS 3 "It had fully formed feathered wings, a perching foot, and a wishbone."

ATTY CARDONA "Was it like a modern bird, then?"

WITNESS 3 "Yes."

ATTY CARDONA "Do some modern birds have wing claws?"

WITNESS 3 "Yes."

ATTY CARDONA "Did some fossil birds have teeth?"

WITNESS 3 "Yes."

ATTY CARDONA "Is it not true that fossil tracks of birds have been found in strata that are dated much older than *Archeopteryx*."[39]

WITNESS 3 "I have heard that."

ATTY CARDONA "Was *Tiktaalik* a fish?"

WITNESS 3 "Yes."

ATTY CARDONA "What features identify it as a fish?"

WITNESS 3 "It had gills, scales, fins, and lived in the water."

ATTY CARDONA "What features were like an amphibian?"

WITNESS 3 It had rays for stiffening in its fins, and probably could support itself on its two front fins and drag itself along like a seal."

ATTY CARDONA "Were its fins connected to its backbone as in land creatures?"

WITNESS 3 "No."

ATTY CARDONA "Did its rear fins show any features that might be considered forerunners of legs?"

WITNESS 3 "No."

ATTY CARDONA "Is it not true that fossil tracks of land creatures were found in Poland in strata that predate *Tiktaalik* just as fossils of birds were found in strata that predate *Archeopteryx*?"[40]

WITNESS 3 "I was not aware of that."

ATTY CARDONA "How then could land creatures have evolved from *Tiktaalik*, or birds from *Archeopteryx*?"

WITNESS 3 "I don't know."

ATTY CARDONA "Is it true that many supposed transitional forms between apes and humans have not survived scrutiny, such as Piltdown Man and Nebraska Man?"

WITNESS 3 "That would be correct."

ATTY CARDONA "When was the first *Australopithecus* fossil discovered?"

WITNESS 3 "The first *Australopithecus afarensis* fossil, called *Lucy*, was discovered in Ethiopia in 1974 by Dr. Donald Johanson."

ATTY CARDONA "How old is *Lucy*?"

ATTY CARDONA "*Lucy* has been dated to be at least three million years old."

ATTY CARDONA "Why has *Lucy* been considered a transitional form between apes and humans?"

WITNESS 3 "Because *Lucy* could evidently walk upright but could also take to the trees if necessary."

ATTY CARDONA "Is it fair to say that nearly all of the features of *Lucy* from the waist upward are like those of chimps, as well as many features of its legs?"

WITNESS 3 "Yes."

ATTY CARDONA "What are its human-like features?"

WITNESS 3 "Its knee and pelvis indicated that it could walk upright."

ATTY CARDONA "Is it not true that Dr. Johanson only found part of its pelvis, and that part had been crushed into about 40 pieces?"

WITNESS 3 "Yes."

ATTY CARDONA "Is it true that the modern pigmy chimp habitually walks upright?"

WITNESS 3 "Yes, although somewhat differently from humans."

ATTY CARDONA "Is it true then that walking upright is not necessarily a human characteristic?"

WITNESS 3 "I suppose it is not."

ATTY CARDONA "Is there any other evidence that Lucy could walk upright?"

WITNESS 3 "Yes. There are the related footprint trails called the Laetoli footprints that have features of creatures walking upright."

ATTY CARDONA "Were the Laetoli footprints discovered near the fossil remains of Lucy?"

WITNESS 3 "No."

ATTY CARDONA "It is true, is it not, that most people, including paleoanthropologists such as Mary Leakey, consider that the Laetoli footprints are remarkably similar to those of modern man?"

WITNESS 3 "Yes."

ATTY CARDONA "Why could they then not have actually been made by humans?"

WITNESS 3 "Because they are located between strata that are 3.6 and 3.8 million years old, respectively, so they are too old to have been made by humans."

ATTY CARDONA "How were the strata dated?"

WITNESS 3 "I believe it was by the potassium-argon radioactive decay method."

ATTY CARDONA "Is it not true that that dating method often gives erroneous results?"

WITNESS 3 "I believe another witness at this trial will discuss that."

ATTY CARDONA "Is it not also true that fossils indistinguishable from modern humans have been discovered that have been dated by similar methods to be up to 4.5 million years old?"[41]

WITNESS 3 "I have read about such claims."

ATTY CARDONA "What other types of fossils have been considered to be intermediates between *Lucy* and modern man."

WITNESS 3 "*Homo habilis, Homo erectus* and archaic *Homo sapiens.*"

ATTY CARDONA "And have you read that so-called *Homo erectus* fossils display consistently the same morphology or form with no change over their supposed two-million-year-old existence?"[42]

WITNESS 3 "Yes."

ATTY CARDONA "Is it fair to say that all *Homo habilis* fossils were contemporary with *Homo erectus* fossils?"[43]

WITNESS 3 "Some people have said that."

ATTY CARDONA "Is it also fair to say that anatomically modern *Homo sapiens*, Neanderthal Man, archaic *Homo sapiens* and *Homo erectus* all lived as contemporaries at one time or another?"[44]

WITNESS 3 "I have heard that also."

ATTY CARDONA "Are you familiar with Mark Ridley, zoologist at Oxford University who studied under Richard Dawkins?"

WITNESS 3 "Yes."

ATTY CARDONA "I submit you to these quotations from Mark Ridley in the *New Scientist Magazine*: '…no real evolutionist, whether gradualist or punctuationist, uses the fossil record as evidence of the theory of evolution as opposed to special creation.' And, 'The evidence for evolution simply does not depend on the fossil record.'[45] So is it not true that the absence of true transitional forms is still an obvious and grave objection to Darwin's theory, as he admitted in his book?"

WITNESS 3 "That is your conclusion."

ATTY CARDONA "Did Darwin believe that humans evolved after wolves and sheep?"

WITNESS 3 "I don't remember that he explicitly said that."

ATTY CARDONA "Would that be a reasonable conclusion from his theory?"

WITNESS 3 "Yes."

ATTY CARDONA "Is it correct that a female wolf each year gives birth to five or six offspring, but a ewe gives birth to just one or maybe two lambs?"

WITNESS 3 "Yes, that is correct."

ATTY CARDONA "Then how could sheep survive in the presence of wolves without protection from humans?"

WITNESS 3 "I don't know right now."

ATTY CARDONA "No further questions for Witness 3."

"For my next witness, I would like to call on Witness 4, representing the work of geneticist John Sanford. Witness 4, please describe the work of Sanford."

WITNESS 4 "John Sanford was a professor of genetics at Cornell University. He was also the inventor of the so-called 'gene gun' for producing genetically modified plants. He is the holder of several patents. Later he collaborated with others in developing extensive computer models of natural selection and published the results in his book *Genetic Entropy*."

ATTY CARDONA "What is the main significance of his results?"

WITNESS 4 "He demonstrated that the so-called Modern Synthesis of Darwinian evolution cannot work. The Modern Synthesis is also called the standard model of evolution."

ATTY CARDONA "To review, that model assumes that evolution works through natural selection on genetic changes produced by random mutations, correct?"

WITNESS 4 "That is correct."

ATTY CARDONA "How did Sanford show that the standard model cannot work?"

WITNESS 4 "There are several reasons. First, mutations produce no new information, but rather act to destroy information that is already present."

ATTY CARDONA "What is information? Is it physical matter?"

WITNESS 4 "No. May I present a simple picture of the difference between physical matter and information?"

ATTY CARDONA "Yes, go ahead."

WITNESS 4 "In the left picture I show an equation written in chalk on a blackboard. That equation conveys some information. In the right picture that equation has been erased, and its information is lost. Nevertheless, the amount of material in the chalk has not changed. Most of the chalk has just fallen to the bottom of the blackboard."

Exhibit 2. *Demonstrating the Nature of Information*

ATTY CARDONA "Why is that important?"

WITNESS 4 "Because the amount of information in DNA is staggering."

ATTY CARDONA "How is information stored in DNA?"

WITNESS 4 "One way is the sequence of simple organic compounds containing nitrogen, carbon and hydrogen that are like letters in a very thick book. Each letter is from an 'alphabet' of four such compounds called nitrogenous bases. Since each of these bases comes with a mating base, the letters are actually 'base pairs.' The DNA sequence called the 'human genome' contains roughly three billion such letters. Even the DNA in single-cell organisms like bacteria typically contain tens of thousands of these letters."

ATTY CARDONA "Is there another way that information is stored in DNA?"

WITNESS 4 "Yes. We are just learning how some parts of the genome can affect other parts of the genome that are far away along the DNA sequence. The study of these features is called epigenetics."

ATTY CARDONA "What does such information do?"

WITNESS 4 "For example, some parts of the DNA sequence can turn on or off the functions of other parts of the DNA in response to changes in the organism's environment."

ATTY CARDONA "How does information originate?"

WITNESS 4 "In the example of the equation on the chalkboard, the information in the equation arises from an intelligent source. The staggering amount of information in the three billion letters of the human genome surely requires an intelligent source."

ATTY CARDONA "Can random mutations produce beneficial effects?"

WITNESS 4 "Beneficial mutations are very rare if they exist at all. Mutations are like random typographical errors in a pre-existing book."

ATTY CARDONA "Can natural selection remove bad mutations?"

WITNESS 4 "The overwhelming majority of mutations are nearly neutral. Like most typographical errors, they don't immediately cause any serious damage. One can usually understand the text in a book even if there are some typographical errors. Only when an important equation or some critical data are changed is there an immediate problem. Similarly, near-neutral mutations cannot be selected out until they eventually accumulate over several generations and cause a noticeable problem."

ATTY CARDONA "How many mutations typically occur in one generation?"

WITNESS 4 "Humans pass on roughly one hundred new mutations to their offspring each generation."

ATTY CARDONA "How does that affect the possibility of natural selection?"

WITNESS 4 "Natural selection only has one chance per generation to select. It cannot select for individual mutations when there are many different simultaneous mutations. It is like a book that exists only in several copies of the old printing, each with a hundred typographical errors. One has to pick the best copy, but even that one will still have many errors. And it gets worse with each new printing when unchanged copies of the previous printing no longer exist."

ATTY CARDONA "Are there other factors that affect natural selection?"

WITNESS 4 "Yes. For example, if one sample of an organism lives in a worse environment than another sample, or if it randomly acquires a bad disease, that sample may be less able to survive even if its inherited mutations are not as bad as in the other sample."

ATTY CARDONA "No further questions of Witness 4. Your witness, Mr. Porter."

ATTY PORTER "Is it not true that some diseases acquire resistance to antibiotics through mutations?"

WITNESS 4 "Yes."

ATTY PORTER "Are they then not examples of beneficial mutations?"

WITNESS 4 "No."

ATTY PORTER "Why is that?"

Witness 4 "Such mutations cause a loss of some function in the microbe causing the disease. That loss makes the microbe less vulnerable to the way that the antibiotic attacks it, but also generally leads to reduced overall fitness of the microbe."

Atty Porter "What about sickle cell anemia, where a mutation in hemoglobin causes a resistance to malaria?"

Witness 4 "The mutated form of hemoglobin is only helpful in resisting malaria. The anemia makes a person generally less fit to survive in a normal environment."

Atty Porter "No further questions of Witness 4."

Judge Jacobsen "Let us break now for lunch. The court is adjourned until this afternoon."

WEDNESDAY NOON

THE WATERING HOLE

As they packed up to leave the courtroom, Brian suggested to Jason, and Witnesses 1 and 4 that they all grab a bite to eat at *The Watering Hole*, just two blocks down from the courthouse. While they enjoyed some spicy Mexican food, they eagerly shared their observations.

"I wonder why Witness 3 didn't cite the standard story of horse transitional forms?" Jason posited.

"Probably because few people believe it anymore," Brian replied. "Even though it's been a staple of science textbooks for many years. You know the issues with it, right?"

"Yeah," said Jason, digging into his burrito. "The ancestor of the horses was supposed to be *Eohippus*, meaning dawn horse. Then they found out that fossils of *Eohippus* looked just like a modern hyrax. Not only that, but fossils of the supposed transitional forms of the horses have all been found in the same strata, along with fossil *Eohippus*.[46] So they would not have been ancestors of each other."

"The Darwinian theory is so flexible it can explain almost anything, isn't it," Witness 1 chimed in.

Witness 4 followed his thought. "That's because it is also so empty and devoid of any concrete mechanisms."

Jason dialed in further. "In particular, how could they explain the origin of metamorphosis of a caterpillar into a butterfly in the cocoon? By the way, that's also a beautiful picture of how our resurrected bodies will look totally different from the ones we have now."

"Brian, why couldn't we bring up so many other evidences for creation, such as irreducible complexity and symbiosis? You know, the fact that organisms like the eye don't work unless all of their complicated subsystems are also working simultaneously. Or the tiny Mexican Melipona bee that is the only insect capable of pollinating a vanilla plant."

"Not only that," said Witness 1. "But the subsystems of an organism have to continue functioning while they are growing. Engineers can design wonderful things, but they don't grow."

"All of that's true," Brian pointed at his watch, "but there's only a limited amount of time to present our arguments. By the way, Witness 4, I've been wanting to ask you how Dr. Sanford managed to survive at a place like Cornell that surely has not been friendly to creation scientists."

"Two reasons, I suppose," Witness 4 began. "First, he'd become rather famous for his inventions like the gene gun and got to be more-or-less financially independent from the university. Secondly, for a long time he too had believed the pantheist idea that evolutionary progress is a principle behind Nature. Even after becoming a Christian, it took him many years to progress from theistic evolutionist to old-earth creationist and finally to a young-earth creation scientist."[47]

"Before I forget," Jason called out. "I want to let you know that my supporters are having a reception for me tonight at 7, at the home of Brandon Taylor at 45 Prospect Street. You're all welcome to come. When we get back to the courtroom, let's tell this afternoon's witnesses also. Brian, can you let tomorrow's witnesses know?"

"Well, it is great to see your supporters doing this for you," Brian affirmed. "But as for me and tomorrow's witnesses, I need to prepare them for their testimonies and do some more prepping myself. Meanwhile, this has definitely been an enjoyable conversation and I hope you enjoyed the delicious food. Before you all take out your credit cards, this is all on me."

WEDNESDAY AFTERNOON

THE COURTROOM

BIOLOGY

Human DNA

JUDGE JACOBSEN "Mr. Cardona, please call your next witness."

ATTY CARDONA "I would like to call Witness 5, representing the work of geneticists Nathaniel Jeanson and Jeffrey Tomkins. Witness 5, please summarize for us the background of these two geneticists."

WITNESS 5 "Dr. Jeanson earned a Bachelor of Science degree in biology and bioinformatics from the University of Wisconsin and a Ph.D. from Harvard in cell and developmental biology. Dr. Tomkins has a Ph.D. in genetics from Clemson University, an MS in plant science and a BS in agriculture education. Drs. Jeanson and Tomkins have collaborated on the genetics of human DNA."

ATTY CARDONA "I understand that Jeanson and Tomkins published some recent work on the testability of theories in genetics. Is that correct?"

WITNESS 5 "Yes. They published an article entitled, 'Genetics Confirms the Recent, Supernatural Creation of Adam and Eve.'"[48]

ATTY CARDONA "What were some of the things that they reported?"

WITNESS 5 "One thing was the falsifiable claim by evolutionists that the human genome mostly consists of 'junk DNA.'"

ATTY CARDONA "Remind us, what is the human genome?"

WITNESS 5 "That is the sequence of all the base pair 'letters' in human DNA."

ATTY CARDONA "Why was most of the genome called 'junk'?"

WITNESS 5 "Soon after the sequence of all the 'letters' that make up the human genome was determined in 2001, they noticed that only some of the blocks of 'letters' in that sequence were codes for making proteins. Those codes are called genes. Since the rest of the genome did not have any obvious function, mainstream geneticists concluded that it was simply junk DNA left over from evolution."

ATTY CARDONA "How was the notion of 'junk DNA' falsified?"

WITNESS 5 "Researchers in the ENCODE project, by 2012, had already discovered functions for most of the human DNA besides the genes that are codes for making proteins."

ATTY CARDONA "What is the ENCODE project?"

WITNESS 5 "ENCODE is a public consortium of researchers in universities and other institutions funded by grants from the National Human Genome Research Institute under the US National Institutes of Health (NIH). It was established in 2003."

ATTY CARDONA "What is the significance of this result about junk DNA?"

WITNESS 5 "It shows that many scientists, without doing any experiments, were quick to make unjustifiable conclusions based on their presuppositions about evolution."

ATTY CARDONA "Are there any other similar examples that you know about?"

WITNESS 5 "Yes. Just as many scientists thought that most of the DNA in the human genome had no function, many scientists thought that parts of the body like the tonsils and the appendix had no function. They called those parts 'vestigial organs.'"

ATTY CARDONA "Why did they call them that?"

Witness 5 "Based on their presuppositions, they assumed those organs were useless vestiges of past evolutionary processes. However, now we know that all these so-called vestigial organs have important functions."[49]

Atty Cardona "Did Drs. Jeanson and Tomkins report any other testable results?"

Witness 5 "Yes, concerning human mitochondrial DNA or 'mtDNA.'"

Atty Cardona "Please explain what is mitochondrial DNA."

Witness 5 "The mtDNA is a small section of DNA found in the energy factories of our cells called the mitochondria. It contains only about 16,000 base pair 'letters,' while the complete human genome contains about three billion such letters. The mtDNA is inherited exclusively from one's mother. By examining mutations in mtDNA, creationists and evolutionists agree that our mtDNA can be traced back to a single woman called 'mitochondrial Eve.'"

Atty Cardona "What then was testable, or predicted?"

Witness 5 "It is known that one mtDNA letter is mutated about once every six human generations, on the average. Assuming that the average time between each generation is 30 years, that means there should be about one letter mutation every 180 years. Evolutionists postulate that the first modern humans lived about 180,000 years ago. So according to the evolutionary model there should be about 1,000 letter changes from 'mitochondrial Eve' to present humans. "The number of differences in the mtDNA between any two humans now should therefore average about 2,000 letters.

"Creationists believe that humans originated roughly 6,000 years ago, and that there were only about ten generations between Eve and the wives of Noah's three sons on the Ark about 4,500 years ago. In that case, the number of differences in the mtDNA between any two humans now should therefore average about 4,500 years divided by 180 years per mutation times two, or 50 letters."

Atty Cardona "What do the actual data show?"

Witness 5 "The most genetically diverse of all human ethnic groups are Africans. Within that population group, the average difference in letters is now about 78. That is close to the prediction from the creationist model, but about 25 times less than the prediction from the evolutionist model."[50] Not only that, but human mtDNA data strongly suggest that all humans are descendants of three women who lived just a few generations after 'mitochondrial Eve.'[51] That is consistent with the Biblical claim that all humans are descended from the wives of Noah's sons."

Atty Cardona "What is the conclusion from these data?"

Witness 5 "The data verify the creationist claim that humans originated only a few thousand years ago."

Atty Cardona "No further questions of Witness 5. Your witness, Mr. Porter."

Atty Porter "No questions for Witness 5; instead I would like to call Witness 6, representing the work of Dennis Venema and similar authors. Witness 6, what is Dr. Venema's background."

Witness 6 "Dr. Venema received a Ph.D. in biology from the University of British Columbia. From 2011 to 2018 he was a Fellow of Biology for the BioLogos Foundation. He is the co-author of *Adam and the Genome*.[52] Recently he has been professor of biology at Trinity Western University."

Atty Porter "Please tell us about the similarity of the DNA of chimpanzees and humans."

Witness 6 "Yes, the genomes of chimps and humans are both known and they match very well."

Atty Porter "Can you indicate roughly how close they match?"

Witness 6 "According to the latest comparisons, the human and chimp genomes are between 95 percent and 98 percent identical."

Atty Porter "What is the significance of this result?"

Witness 6 "The similarity of the genomes indicates that chimpanzees and humans are closely related."

Atty Porter "Are there any significant differences in the DNA between two different humans?"

Witness 6 "The average measured difference is about 0.1 percent. The total genome consists of three billion base pairs, commonly referred to as 'letters.' In comparing two different humans, we expect that the average difference would be twice the total mutations in each individual, since the mutations would almost always be different in the generations leading to each. So the observed difference corresponds to 0.1 percent times six billion letters, or six million letters."

Atty Porter "How fast does human DNA mutate from one generation to the next?"

Witness 6 "The mutation rate is between 60 and 100 mutations per generation."

Atty Porter "So, if humans began with a single couple, such as Adam and Eve, how long ago would Adam and Eve have lived?"

Witness 6 "Even with 100 mutations per generation, and six million total mutations, it would take 60,000 generations. If the average time between generations were only 20 years, that would still mean that 1.2 million years would be required. If the average mutation rate were 60 per generation and the time between generations were 30 years on average, then 100,000 generations and 3 million years would be required."

Atty Porter "That amount of time is much greater than the creationists' estimate of 6,000 years from Adam and Eve to the present, correct?"

Witness 6 "Yes."

Atty Porter "What is your conclusion from this discrepancy?"

Witness 6 "Since creationists claim that Adam and Eve lived at the beginning of creation, this discrepancy disproves the creationists' claim that the earth is young."

Atty Porter "No further questions for Witness 6. Your witness, Mr. Cardona."

Atty Cardona "Witness 6, is it not true that claims were made that the human and chimp genomes are 99 percent identical?"

Witness 6 "Yes, that is true."

Atty Cardona "Why then is it your testimony now that the genomes are only 95 percent to 98 percent identical?"[53]

Witness 6 "The work in 2005 compared only genes. Genes are only the part of the genome that provides the code for making proteins."

Atty Cardona "Is it fair to say that all these comparisons omitted regions of the genomes that could not be compared?"

Witness 6 "Yes."

Atty Cardona "Is it true that those omitted regions accounted for roughly 6 percent of the genomes?"

Witness 6 "It is not possible to align all the regions in the genomes."

Atty Cardona "Is it fair to say then then, at most 90 percent of the genomes are identical?"[54]

Witness 6 "I can't verify that."

Atty Cardona "If the human and chimp genomes are each roughly three billion base pair letters long, then a 10 percent difference would amount to 300 million letters, correct?"

Witness 6 "In that case, yes."

Atty Cardona "Would the evolution model predict such a large difference between chimps and humans?"

Witness 6 "If the human lineage branched off from the chimpanzee lineage a long time ago, yes."

ATTY CARDONA "How long ago would that be?"

WITNESS 6 "Well, if we take your 300 million letter difference and assume 100 mutations per generation, that would be three million generations, or perhaps 60 to 90 million years."

ATTY CARDONA "Did the evolution model originally predict a much shorter time?"

WITNESS 6 "Yes."

ATTY CARDONA "Was the original prediction in 2012 about 3 to 6 million years?"

WITNESS 6 "Yes."

ATTY CARDONA "And then the prediction was revised in 2014 to 13 million years?"[55]

WITNESS 6 "I heard that."

ATTY CARDONA "Why the big discrepancy between 60 to 90 million years or even 13 million years and 3 to 6 million years?"

WITNESS 6 "Well, first of all your claim of only 90 percent similarity between chimp and human genomes. And science is self-correcting."

ATTY CARDONA "Or would it be that evolutionists have been retrofitting the predictions to the facts?"

ATTY PORTER "Objection, your honor. The question assumes the answer."

JUDGE JACOBSEN "Objection sustained."

ATTY CARDONA "It is true, is it not, that genes are the parts of the genome that provide the information for making proteins?"

WITNESS 6 "Yes."

ATTY CARDONA "Is it also true that many genes in kangaroos are virtually identical to those in humans?"

WITNESS 6 "I was not aware of that."

ATTY CARDONA "Allow me to insert a news article link into the record, your honor."

JUDGE JACOBSEN "What is the source of the article?"

ATTY CARDONA "It is a Reuters news article titled, 'Kangaroo genes close to humans,' dated November 2008."[56]

JUDGE JACOBSEN "Yes, go ahead."

ATTY CARDONA "In the evolutionary model, are kangaroos ancestors of humans?"

WITNESS 6 "No."

ATTY CARDONA "Is it not true, Witness 6, that many proteins in different animals are the same?"

WITNESS 6 "Yes."

ATTY CARDONA "Is it correct to say then that similarity in genes and DNA can indicate common design rather than common ancestry?"

WITNESS 6 "That's your interpretation."

ATTY CARDONA "But is it a wrong interpretation?"

WITNESS 6 "Scientists don't accept that interpretation."

ATTY CARDONA "How do such scientists know that interpretation is not correct?"

WITNESS 6 "Because it doesn't make sense."

ATTY CARDONA "Why doesn't it make sense?"

WITNESS 6 "You would have to ask them."

ATTY CARDONA "Is it not because such scientists reject a supernatural Designer and Creator?"

WITNESS 6 "That would not be the only reason."

ATTY CARDONA "But would it be one of the reasons?"

WITNESS 6 "I suppose it would."

Atty Cardona "Your conclusion about the origin of a 0.1 percent average difference in the genome between two humans is based on the accumulation of mutations, correct?"

Witness 6 "Yes."

Atty Cardona "Your conclusion also assumes that there would be no differences in the DNA of a hypothetical Adam and Eve, correct?"

Witness 6 "That is logical."

Atty Cardona "The human genome consists of 23 regions called chromosomes, correct?"

Witness 6 "Of course."

Atty Cardona "And each offspring contains two copies of the 23 chromosomes, one copy from the mother and one copy from the father, correct?"

Witness 6 "Yes, that is correct."

Atty Cardona "Then each cell in the human body consists of roughly three billion DNA letters, correct?"

Witness 6 "Correct. Except that red blood cells contain no nucleus and hence no DNA."

Atty Cardona "So it's conceivable that the content of the chromosomes inherited by the offspring from Adam could have been much different from the chromosomes inherited from Eve?"

Witness 6 "I suppose so."

Atty Cardona "Is it not true that the DNA in the inherited chromosomes could be shuffled by at least two processes called recombination and gene conversion?"

Witness 6 "Yes, that is true."

Atty Cardona "Then each offspring of Adam and Eve could have unique and diverse DNA, correct?"

Witness 6 "I suppose so."

ATTY CARDONA "Is it fair to say that such diversity could be much greater than the diversity caused by mutations in 6000 years?"

WITNESS 6 "Possibly."

ATTY CARDONA "Is it also fair to say that this diversity could account for the 0.1 percent average difference in the DNA between two humans today?"

WITNESS 6 "That's hard to say."

ATTY CARDONA "No further questions, your honor.

JUDGE JACOBSEN "Mr. Cardona, I believe that you wish to proceed with witnesses concerning geology next, is that correct?"

ATTY CARDONA "Yes, beginning with the fossil record."

JUDGE JACOBSEN "I think we have enough time for one more witness this afternoon, but first let's take a short fifteen-minute break."

A SHORT BREAK

Jason got up and went over to Witnesses 5 and 7 to invite them to the evening's reception at Brandon's house. A balding older man in a tweed suit stood nearby and caught some of their conversation.

"I'm a reporter for the Dale County News-Express," the man said to Jason. "Would you mind if I came to your reception? My name is Douglas Thomason."

Jason replied, "Ah yes, I saw your piece on the trial this morning."

"Well, I hope I didn't offend you too much," Thomason ventured. "No problem. We'll be happy to have you join us. I understand there will only be juice, herb teas and light snacks, though. Let me send the address to your phone."

GEOLOGY

The Fossil Record

JUDGE JACOBSEN "The court is back in session. Mr. Cardona, please call your next witness."

ATTY CARDONA "My witness this afternoon concerning the fossils will be representing the work of Dr. John Morris and Mr. Frank Sherwin. Witness 7, please describe their background."

WITNESS 7 "Dr. Morris received a doctorate in geological engineering from the University of Oklahoma in 1980. He was president of the Institute for Creation Research from 1996 to 2010. Frank Sherwin received a master's degree in zoology in 1985 and an honorary doctorate from Pensacola Christian University. Morris and Sherwin were co-authors of *The Fossil Record*."

ATTY CARDONA "Please tell us what is required for fossils to form."

WITNESS 7 "Rapid burial and quick hardening are required. Otherwise, scavengers and bacteria will soon consume the dead plant or animal."

ATTY CARDONA "What is the origin of fossils?"

WITNESS 7 "Worldwide, 95 percent of all fossils have a marine origin. Less than 5 percent of all fossils are plants, trees and algae, while less than 1 of all fossils are vertebrates, including land animals."[57]

ATTY CARDONA "What is the significance of the large proportion of marine fossils?"

WITNESS 7 "Marine fossils are found in all of the geologic layers, even near the top of Mt. Everest.[58] That is consistent with burial by multiple wide-scale tsunami-like water flows separated by successive runoffs."

Atty Cardona "Do we see other fossil evidence of such water flows?"

Witness 7 "Yes. For example, in the large Morrison Formation covering much of the American West, we see huge graveyards of dinosaurs mixed with clams and saltwater fish. The dinosaurs must have been transported from elsewhere, since at the location of their fossils there is no indication of any sources of food for them to eat. The clams and saltwater fish also had to come from a faraway ocean."[59]

Atty Cardona "What are the characteristics of the fossil record?"

Witness 7 "From the oldest to the more recent geologic layers, except for marine fossils, one notices: (1) sudden appearance of new life forms, followed by (2) absence of any change in those life forms, and finally, (3) disappearance of those life forms."

Atty Cardona "What can one conclude from this situation?"

Witness 7 "There is no indication of gradual change such as required by evolution. Rather, the evidence is consistent with successive catastrophic water flows reaching higher and higher elevations and encountering successive varieties of life."

Atty Cardona "Please describe the so-called geologic column."

Witness 7 "The geologic column is a model of the geologic layers from oldest to youngest. Such a column does not actually exist at any one location on the earth, but it does display the relative age of the layers where they are found. May I show a representative drawing of such a column?"

Atty Cardona "Yes, please. I will enter it into the record. What are the times shown on that drawing?"

The Geologic Column

ERA	PERIOD	EPOCH	SUCCESSION OF LIFE
CENOZOIC *recent life*	**QUATERNARY** 0-1 Million Years Rise of Man	Recent Pleisto- cene	
	TERTIARY 62 Million Years Rise of Mammals	Pliocene Miocene Oligocene Eocene	
MESOZOIC *middle life*	**CRETACEOUS** 72 Million Years Modern seed bearing plants. Dinosaurs		
	JURASSIC 46 Million Years First birds		
	TRIASSIC 49 Million Years Cycads, first dinosaurs		
PALEOZOIC *ancient life*	**PERMIAN** 50 Million Years First reptiles		
	PENNSYLVANIAN 30 Million Years First insects	*Carboniferous*	
	MISSISSIPPIAN 35 Million Years Many crinoids		
	DEVONIAN 60 Million Years First seed plants, cartilage fish		
	SILURIAN 20 Million Years Earliest land animals		
	ORDOVICIAN 75 Million Years Early bony fish		
	CAMBRIAN 100 Million Years Invertebrate animals, Brachiopods, Trilobites		
	PRECAMBRIAN Very few fossils present (bacteria-algae-pollen?)		

Exhibit 3. *The Standard Geologic Column*

Witness 7 "Times listed such as '62 million years' in the Tertiary period refer to durations of the periods according to assumptions of mainstream geologists. I understand that other witnesses will testify concerning the reliability of those assumptions."

Atty Cardona "Please tell us what is the so-called Cambrian explosion?"

Witness 7 "Fossils representative of all groups of animals are found abruptly in the Cambrian geologic layer. Below that layer only fossils of single-celled organisms are found."

Atty Cardona "Is there any evidence of evolutionary change in the Cambrian fossils?"

Witness 7 "No. The gaps between the fossils in the Cambrian layer mirror the gaps seen between animals living today."

Atty Cardona "Please explain what is a 'living fossil.'"

Witness 7 "A living fossil is one that looks the same as a creature living today."

Atty Cardona "Where are 'living fossils' found?"

Witness 7 "'Living fossils' are found in all layers of the geologic column."

Atty Cardona "What are some examples?"

Witness 7 "Stromatolites from Precambrian strata, horseshoe crabs, coelacanth fish, sea lilies from the Mississippian layer, dragonflies from the Jurassic, crocodiles, sycamore leaves from the Eocene layer, wasps from the Oligocene and dragonfly nymphs from the Miocene."[60]

Atty Cardona "What is significant about these 'living fossils'?"

Witness 7 "They are further evidence that no evolution has occurred over all the time represented in the geologic column."

Atty Cardona "Do any of the fossils themselves indicate rapid burial?"

Witness 7 "Yes, there is a fly fossilized with the eggs it just laid, a fossil ichthyosaur in the process of giving birth and fossils of fish in the process of eating other fish.[61] Here is a photo of one of those."

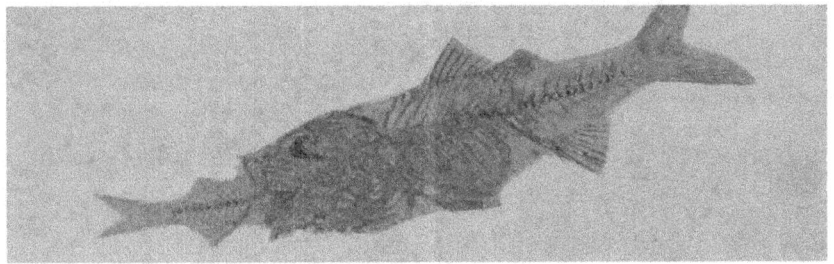

Exhibit 4. *Fossil of a fish eating another fish*

ATTY CARDONA "Why don't we see dinosaurs alive today?"

WITNESS 7 "Many life forms have gone extinct over time. Even nowadays, many species die out each year. Nevertheless, there is evidence that dinosaurs and humans lived together not long ago."

ATTY CARDONA "What would such evidence be?"

WITNESS 7 "Many cultures have legends and drawings of what they called dragons, some of which closely resemble particular dinosaurs known from fossils."

ATTY CARDONA "Is there other evidence that dinosaurs lived not long ago?"

WITNESS 7 "Yes. Recently soft tissue has been found in a large number of fossils of dinosaurs and other animals."

ATTY CARDONA "What types of soft tissue were found?"

WITNESS 7 "Proteins such as collagen and blood vessels."

ATTY CARDONA "Have any explanations been given concerning how such soft tissue could be preserved for millions of years?"

WITNESS 7 "Yes. Environments with lack of oxygen and/or microbes that cause decay, some mechanisms to shelter collagens, and preservation with iron solutions have been proposed."

ATTY CARDONA "Do those explanations seem like desperate attempts to continue believing that dinosaur fossils are tens of millions of years old?"

ATTY PORTER "Objection, your honor."

JUDGE JACOBSEN "Objection sustained."

ATTY CARDONA "Have those explanations been refuted?"

WITNESS 7 "Yes, in particular by the work of Dr. Kevin Anderson."[62]

ATTY CARDONA "Would one find further evidence that dinosaur fossils are young?"

WITNESS 7 "Yes. Significant levels of radioactive carbon 14 have recently been measured in dinosaur fossils."[63]

ATTY CARDONA "Why does the presence of carbon 14 indicate a young age?"

WITNESS 7 "Carbon 14 decays so rapidly that none should be measurable after about 80,000 years. I understand that another witness will have something to say about dating with carbon 14."

ATTY CARDONA "What are polystrate fossils?"

WITNESS 7 "They are fossilized trees that are seen penetrating several geologic layers, or strata. Some single trees pass through several layers of coal, shale and limestone."

ATTY CARDONA "How do they form?"

WITNESS 7 "Silica, similar to sand, dissolved in hot water can rapidly surround, fill in, or replace the wood cells in a dead tree. The water itself may be percolating through volcanic ash. This process transforms the tree basically into a rock with the shape of the original tree. The process is called petrification."

ATTY CARDONA "Are groups of polystrate trees often referred to as petrified forests?"

WITNESS 7 "Yes."

ATTY CARDONA "Can petrification occur today?"

WITNESS 7 "Yes, under the right conditions. For example, a split-rail fencepost was partially buried in volcanic ash in Washington state in the mid-1800s. While the upper part of the post subsequently rotted, the below-ground portion petrified."[64]

ATTY CARDONA "How do we know that trees in petrified forests were fossilized rapidly?"

WITNESS 7 "The trees could not have been fossilized slowly in multiple layers, since the partially exposed portions of the trees would have rotted before the next layers were deposited."

ATTY CARDONA "How do we know that such trees did not just grow where their fossils are found?"

WITNESS 7 "Matching tree rings seen in nearby fossilized trees often occur at different elevations in the strata."[65]

ATTY CARDONA "No further questions at this time. Your witness, Mr. Porter."

ATTY PORTER "Witness 7, According to creationists, all the basic life forms were created during the time described in Genesis 1, correct?"

WITNESS 7 "Yes."

ATTY PORTER "And the so-called Noah's Flood is described in Genesis chapters 7 and 8, correct?"

WITNESS 7 "Correct."

ATTY PORTER "Why then do we see stromatolite fossils in Precambrian strata but not, for example, any fish fossils there?"

WITNESS 7 "Flood geologists consider that most Precambrian strata were created on Day 3 of Genesis when solid material called "dry land" appeared. Before that there was only water. Stromatolites are single-celled organisms that probably were created along with grass and trees also on Day 3. God created fish later on Day 5."

ATTY PORTER "Is it true that creationists say there is no evidence of any ancestors of the fossils found in the so-called Cambrian explosion?"

WITNESS 7 "That is true."

ATTY PORTER "Is it not also true that Cambrian fossils generally have hard shells?"

WITNESS 7 "Yes, that is true."

ATTY PORTER "And are hard-shelled creatures more easily fossilized than those without shells?"

WITNESS 7 "In general, I suppose so."

ATTY PORTER "Is it not logical then that the ancestors of the creatures seen in Cambrian fossils would be simpler, have no shells, and therefore not be found in Precambrian strata?"

WITNESS 7 "That might seem logical, but it does not hold up to the evidence."

ATTY PORTER "Why is that?"

WITNESS 7 "We know that even fossils of single-celled organisms such as stromatolites could be preserved in Precambrian strata. Fossils of some more complicated creatures could surely have been preserved had they existed. Yet I know of no example in the Precambrian strata of any fossils that could remotely be considered ancestors of the multitudes of creatures fossilized in Cambrian strata."

ATTY PORTER "Concerning fossils buried rapidly, such as a fish in the process of eating another fish, must they be formed in a flood, or could they not be formed from the fallout from a volcanic eruption, or drifting into water with insufficient oxygen?"

WITNESS 7 "Fossil formation requires rapid and rather deep burial to minimize the supply of oxygen and water so that bacteria cannot disintegrate the creature."

ATTY PORTER "We've already established that, according to creationists, all the basic life forms were created during the time described in Genesis 1, correct?"

WITNESS 7 "Yes."

ATTY PORTER "Is it true that in the Grand Canyon there are no fossils of plants, oak and maple trees, snakes, turtles, kangaroos, hawks, monkeys or freshwater fish?"

WITNESS 7 "Yes, that is true."

ATTY PORTER "If there were a worldwide flood that covered the Earth, why wouldn't such fossils be seen in the Grand Canyon?"

WITNESS 7 "The uppermost layer in the Grand Canyon, at the Canyon rim, is Kaibab limestone. Even though its elevation now is much above sea level, it is likely that this layer was formed under the shallow sea surrounding the continents that then existed. Hence this layer and all other layers lower in the Grand Canyon only contain fossils of salt water marine creatures. Only later in Noah's flood did the water level rise over higher land that then existed. And even later the Kaibab layer was uplifted. I understand that another witness will have more to say about that uplifting."

ATTY PORTER "How long ago do creationists believe Noah lived?"

WITNESS 7 "Based on genealogies in Genesis, roughly 4,500 years ago."

ATTY PORTER "Is it not true that creationists have recently been claiming rapid speciation of the animals supposedly on Noah's Ark?"

WITNESS 7 "Yes."

ATTY PORTER "Why do they have to claim that?"

WITNESS 7 "The account of the worldwide flood in Genesis mentions that Noah took on the Ark only two of some kinds of animals and seven of other kinds. After leaving the Ark, these kinds would need to proliferate within several thousand years into the multitude of species seen today."

ATTY PORTER "Is that not an example of rapid evolution?"

WITNESS 7 "No. The new species were always derived from an animal of the same kind, such as the dog kind. We also know, for example, that breeders have created a huge variety of new dog species in a few hundred years."

ATTY PORTER "How could rapid speciation occur without human intervention?"

WITNESS 7 "Geneticists have recently found that organisms contain elaborate built-in systems that rapidly react to changes in their environment. For example, a genetic overlay of DNA in the genome contains so-called epigenetic switches that can turn on or off the functions of genes in response to the environment. The changes can be hereditary. As animals spread out from the Ark, they would encounter new environments that would trigger these switches, as well as other changes to the genome. The result would be different species better adapted to the various new environments."

ATTY PORTER "If dinosaurs lived at the same time as humans, why are they not mentioned in the Bible?"

WITNESS 7 "The word 'dinosaur' was first coined in 1841, long after the first English Bibles. Nevertheless, the description a of beast called Behemoth in the book of Job closely corresponds to a variety of dinosaur seen in fossils."

ATTY PORTER "No further questions."

JUDGE JACOBSEN "Then the court is adjourned until tomorrow morning."

Jason turned to Brian and said, "I hope you have a good evening prepping tomorrow's witnesses."

"I'm sure I will," Brian nodded. "I'm meeting them at the restaurant next to my office first. But I'd have been happy to be at your reception if I could."

WEDNESDAY EVENING

THE HOME OF BRANDON TAYLOR

Jason walked up to the door of Brandon Taylor's house and rang the bell. A middle-aged gentleman greeted him and welcomed him inside. Brandon was exceptionally fit for his age, with a full head of salt and pepper hair. He was a surgeon at a distinguished hospital and had been praying for Jason and watching the case closely.

"I apologize for being a few minutes late," Jason explained. "I spent a few extra minutes with Carol and Collin after supper."

"No problem. You've had quite a week, and everyone is excited to welcome you," Brandon responded cheerfully. As they walked into the next room, some guests greeted him with a rendition of "He's a Jolly Good Fellow" and applause.

His student, Peter Benson came up to him and said, "I really miss you, Mr. Radcliffe. The new teacher isn't the same. These are my parents."

"We met you at parents' night," his parents ventured, "and we want to thank you for teaching Peter. Especially he learned a lot from comparing the opposing books on geology that he borrowed from you."

"As a matter of fact, those two books will be a big part of tomorrow morning's testimonies," Jason replied. "And we certainly hope that the judge sees how superior the creation science book is."

Jason then looked around and noticed reporter Thomason chatting in a corner with Witness 4. Jason went over to listen and heard Thomason saying, "You know, I've always wondered about a question that the attorney for the prosecution, Williams Jennings Bryan, couldn't answer at the famous Scopes Trial a hundred years ago.

Clarence Darrow, the defense attorney, asked him, 'Where did Cain get his wife?' and Bryan was stumped."

"Yes," Witness 4 replied, "most people still don't know how to answer that question, but it's really quite simple."

"How so?"

"Well, first of all, Genesis chapter 5 says that Adam had sons and daughters."

"But surely Cain couldn't marry his sister," Thomason persisted.

"Why not?" Witness 4 parried.

"It's not allowed, since they probably would have had the same mutations, and their children would die right away."

"You forget," Witness 4 said, "that Adam and Eve were created perfect, with no mutations. Their chromosomes would have also been much different from each other, so that much diversity could be present in their offspring, who inherited one set of chromosomes from each parent. Hence their children would only have had a few mutations, and surely different ones at that. It's only many generations later that the Bible forbade brothers and sisters to marry, after many mutations had accumulated."

"Oh, I see," Thomason said, "Thank you. That's bothered me for a long time."

"One more question, if you will, where did the races come from?"

"Surely we are all one race, since we all are descended from Adam through Noah," Witness 4 responded. "Not like Darwin said, that different people groups, or races as he called them, were descended from different types of apes. A lot of racist theories originated from Darwin's views."

"But how then did different skin colors and eye features come about?"

"Skin color is largely due to the amount of melanin pigment we have in our skin, and that is determined by genetics. We all have some melanin. If you hold up a sheet of white paper to the skin of a so-called white person, you will see that his skin isn't really white."

Brandon's loud voice then interrupted all the conversations in the room. "Everyone, please listen up! I have an announcement to make."

When the crowd hushed down, Brandon continued, "Our witnesses in the trial today have gotten together and agreed that they all will pay their own travel expenses for this trial so they will not be a burden for Jason."

"Here, here!" shouted one of the visitors, and another said, "Praise God!"

Brandon next turned to his wife and said, "Please dear, tell us the latest results of the crowdfunding."

She replied, "As of this afternoon, we're now up to 61,000 dollars. Meanwhile, please help yourself to more snacks and tea."

"There's plenty of hot water and beverages in the kitchen," Jason interjected. "Thank you all for your generosity and support. It really means a lot to our family."

"But—"Thomason turned back to Witness 4 and went on, "how come some people groups look darker than others?"

"Well, at the tower of Babel people groups were separated by family lines and language and then migrated to different locations. Of those who migrated to colder climates, ones with darker skin could not get as much vitamin D unless they ate a lot of fish, since melanin acts as a sunblock. Of those who migrated to warmer climates, the ones with lighter skin would be more prone to cancers caused by ultraviolet radiation in sunlight since they had less melanin in their skin. So the relative climates would have sorted out the people better able to adapt to them."

Witness 4 continued, "Nevertheless, even today, children of parents with genes from different people groups can be remarkably different. In some cases, one twin can have very light skin while the other twin can have very dark skin."[66]

"Very interesting," Thomason concluded. "Thanks."

THURSDAY MORNING

THE COURTHOUSE CAFETERIA

Brian looked up from his phone and asked Jason, "How did it go yesterday evening?"

"It was really nice. Everyone was very supportive, and the witnesses there even said that they would pay for their own travel expenses."

"That's truly remarkable, isn't it," Brian said. "You know, the witnesses I worked with last evening volunteered the same thing."

"Praise God," Jason responded. "Not only that, but Mr. Thomason, the reporter, actually showed up, and one of our witnesses answered some of his questions. I stayed up pretty late, so I'm a bit tired this morning. The intensity of this trial must be getting to me a little also. How about you, Brian? You're doing all the work."

"I'm pretty used to the trial routine. The adrenaline keeps me going. You know, for a courthouse cafeteria these pastries aren't bad at all. By the way, did you see anything from Thomason today?"

"Yes, as a matter of fact, he had a piece titled, 'Creationists in Teacher Trial Predict Death by Mutations.' Not a very cheery thought, but true enough for humans I suppose in the long term. Even in the short term, mutations cause us to deteriorate with age. And…let's see…oh, here's something from the other reporter, Manning. The first line of his story reads, 'Creationist witnesses are made to look like fossils as scientists debunk their arguments." Same old Manning, I guess. Should we go now?"

"Yes, the trial starts again in a few minutes. We've got some really strong testimonies today."

THURSDAY MORNING

THE COURTROOM

JUDGE JACOBSEN "Good morning, all. The court is back in session. Today we will consider more evidences from geology. Remember that the court is considering the plaintiff's claim that a plain reading of Genesis is a reliable description of the world's physical origins. Mr. Cardona, you may call your first witness."

GEOLOGY

The Geologic Strata

ATTY CARDONA "Now I would like to call witness Witness 8, representing the geologic work of Dr. Steve Austin, Dr. Tim Clarey, Dr. Andrew Snelling, Dr. John Whitmore and Dr. Ron Neller. Witness 8, please tell us a little bit about the background of these geologists."

WITNESS 8 "Yes. These all have extensive experience in geology. Dr. Austin received his Ph.D. in geology from Pennsylvania State University, and extensively explored regions around Mount Saint Helens in Washington state after its volcanic eruption. He became a professor of geology at Cedarville University.

"Dr. Clarey received his Ph.D. in geology from Western Michigan University, worked several years developing oil drilling prospects for Chevron USA, and recently has extensively studied data from worldwide stratigraphic columns. Dr. Andrew Snelling earned a Ph.D. in geology from the University of Sydney, worked for several years as a field, mine and research geologist for companies in Australia, and has extensively studied features of the strata in the Grand Canyon.

"Dr. John Whitmore earned his Ph.D. from Loma Linda University, founded the geology program at Cedarville University and has been a professor there. Dr. Ron Neller has a Ph.D. in fluvial geomorphology. He held lecturing and research positions at universities in Australia, Finland, and Hong Kong, and undertook landscape studies in Australia, China, Finland, Peru, the Pacific Islands, and Libya."

ATTY CARDONA "Please tell us what would be the source of water for a worldwide Flood."

WITNESS 8 "The account in the book of Genesis states that 'the fountains of the great deep were broken up' at the start of the Flood in Noah's time. It is now known that the Earth's mantle contains vast amounts of trapped water."[67]

ATTY CARDONA "Is there evidence that such water burst forth to cause such a Flood?"

WITNESS 8 "Yes. There is evidence that massive volcanic eruptions occurred at the time when Cambrian rocks were formed. Those are the oldest rocks containing marine vertebrate fossils and so would correspond to the beginning of the Flood. In central North America alone, roughly two million cubic kilometers of lava was deposited at that time. Massive amounts of hydrothermal water could easily have been expelled from the upper mantle during and after the eruption of these lava flows."[68]

ATTY CARDONA "What is 'fluvial geomorphology'?"

WITNESS 8 "That is the study of how features of the earth's surface are formed by floods."

ATTY CARDONA "Please begin by summarizing some geologic evidence for a worldwide flood."

WITNESS 8 "About 70 percent of the land surface of the earth is covered by layers of sedimentary rock. It is generally acknowledged that liquid flows are required to form sedimentary layers. The boundaries of similar sedimentary layers called strata extend across all the major continents. The major boundaries define six so-called megasequences."

ATTY CARDONA "How were these boundaries determined?"

WITNESS 8 "Models of 3000 stratigraphic columns have been constructed across six continents using published geological data.[69] Such data included observations of exposed strata, cores taken from deep boreholes, and seismic measurements of reflections from the various layers. Successful correlations of the sequences of rock types between all the columns confirmed the existence of worldwide strata each laid down at the same time. Similar correlations could be made from the fossils contained in the strata."

ATTY CARDONA "How do these megasequences relate to the supposed Flood at Noah's time?"

WITNESS 8 "Each megasequence represents a major advance of ocean water, followed by a slight drop in water level before a new megasequence advanced on top of the previous one."

ATTY CARDONA "Was there a particular source of water that could have contributed to the sedimentary flows in these megasequences?"

WITNESS 8 "Yes. During the Flood year, the pre-Flood ocean basins were being pushed up from below as new seafloor was rapidly being created."

ATTY CARDONA "What is an example of widespread strata in these megasequences?"

WITNESS 8 "Black shale deposits were formed nearly simultaneously in the Devonian geologic period across North America and even globally."[70]

ATTY CARDONA "What is shale?"

WITNESS 8 "Shale is soft sedimentary rock formed from mud. Organic materials such as oil and natural gas are found in shales."

ATTY CARDONA "What is the standard model for shale formation?"

WITNESS 8 "Mainstream geologists claim that shale formation required stagnant water and extremely low oxygen to preserve the organic material."

ATTY CARDONA "Why is the Flood a better explanation for shale formation?"

WITNESS 8 "Firstly, most shale exists in laminations. Only moving water can produce such laminations. Secondly, rapid burial preserves organic material faster than it can be consumed by bacteria. Thirdly, the shale layers exist all over the world."[71]

ATTY CARDONA "How do we know that organic material is rapidly consumed by bacteria?"

WITNESS 8 "We have seen bacteria rapidly consume huge oil spills, such as in the Gulf of Mexico in 2010.[72] We also know that bacteria exist even at great depths in the ground."[73]

ATTY CARDONA "Does that have further significance?"

WITNESS 8 "Yes, it is evidence that oil could not be millions of years old."

ATTY CARDONA "How do we know that oil can form rapidly?"

WITNESS 8 "In 2013, engineers transformed harvested algae into crude oil in less than one hour. Other laboratory experiments have demonstrated formation of crude oil chemicals in as little as 12 hours."[74]

ATTY CARDONA "Can coal also be formed rapidly?"

WITNESS 8 "Yes."

ATTY CARDONA "How do we know that?"

WITNESS 8 "For example, an avalanche of rock and mud from the eruption of Mount Saint Helens in 1980, in Washington state, slammed into nearby Spirit Lake, causing water to rise up and scour a mountain slope on the opposite side of the lake. The rise and fall of the water swept all the trees off that slope and down into the lake. The scouring action removed all the bark from those trees. The bark then fell to the bottom of the lake along with other tree remnants and formed peat about a meter thick. A subsequent volcanic eruption could readily bury the peat under hot lava or ash and form coal."[75]

ATTY CARDONA "What is the standard model for coal formation?"

WITNESS 8 "Mainstream geologists claim that coal contains plants that accumulated in freshwater swamps or peat bogs over many thousands of years."

ATTY CARDONA "Why is the Flood a better model for coal formation?"

WITNESS 8 "Firstly, there are no roots in coal or in the layers under coal such as would be expected if the coal were formed in place in a swamp. Today's swamp peat is thoroughly penetrated with roots. Secondly, examination of coal shows the outline of bark, such as was deposited at the bottom of Spirit Lake near Mount Saint Helens. Thirdly, coal seams can be 100 to 300 feet thick, extend over tens of miles and have flat tops and bottoms. Layers of marine sediment are sometimes seen interspersed between flat coal layers."[76]

ATTY CARDONA "What other features of Flood geology can be seen in the aftermath of the eruption of Mount Saint Helens?"

WITNESS 8 "We see rapid formation of strata and canyons, for example. A couple of years after the main eruption, mud flows from a subsequent eruption carved out a canyon looking like a miniature Grand Canyon. These mud flows exposed distinct layers of sedimentary rocks that were deposited in one day during the main eruption.

I have a photo of these layers. Notice that the vertical extent of these layers is much greater than that of the person in the photo."[77]

Exhibit 5. *Sedimentary layers in a canyon formed at Mount Saint Helens*

ATTY CARDONA "I will insert the photo into the record."

ATTY CARDONA "Concerning canyons, is there a particular feature of interest in the Grand Canyon?"

WITNESS 8 "Yes. For example, there are bends in the bottom sedimentary layer of the Grand Canyon, the Tapeats Sandstone. These bends are folds in the rock that can be as much as 90 degrees near the eastern end of the Canyon. May I show a representative photo?"

ATTY CARDONA "Yes, go ahead. Can you explain how such a fold was formed?"

Exhibit 6. *90-degree fold in the Tapeats Sandstone layer at the Grand Canyon. Note the man standing in the middle of the photo.*[78]

WITNESS 8 "The Biblical flood could have laid down the Tapeats Sandstone in its first month, followed by deposition of the other sedimentary layers. All these layers would have still been wet and relatively soft after about a year under the flood waters. At that time they were rapidly uplifted to form the Kaibab plateau now at the east end of the Canyon. The rapid uplift also bent the Tapeats Sandstone layer smoothly without shattering. The rock subsequently dried out and hardened."

ATTY CARDONA "What caused the uplift in the plateau?"

WITNESS 8 "It is generally agreed that movement of parts of the earth's crust called tectonic plates caused the uplift. There is just disagreement about how fast those plates moved in the past."

ATTY CARDONA "What is the standard geological explanation of the rock folds?"

WITNESS 8 "Evolutionary geologists believe the Tapeats Sandstone was deposited around 500 million years ago. For about the next 450 million years, the sandstone was compressed and hardened as other sediment layers were deposited on top of it. Then roughly 50 million years ago these layers were bent as the plateau was lifted up. They believe that the hardened sandstone was made flexible like Play-Doh by the pressure and heat of the deep burial and the subsequent earth movements so it would bend smoothly."

ATTY CARDONA "What is the main consequence of the standard explanation?"

WITNESS 8 "The required pressure and heat should have metamorphosed the original sedimentary rock layers, changing the minerals, their crystal shapes, and the rock textures."

ATTY CARDONA "What was actually observed?"

WITNESS 8 "Extensive examination under microscopes of 25 samples from the Tapeats Sandstone in the Grand Canyon showed no evidence of any metamorphic changes in the sandstone or its minerals. These rocks came both from the folds and from miles away from the folds."[79]

ATTY CARDONA "What then is the conclusion from these observations?"

WITNESS 8 "The observations confirm the flood model and refute the explanations of evolutionary geologists."

ATTY CARDONA "Can you tell us anything about observations of erosion in the Grand Canyon strata?"

WITNESS 8 "The boundaries between the Grand Canyon layers are often extremely flat and show minimal evidence of erosion."

ATTY CARDONA "Is that a problem for the standard model of formation of those layers?"

WITNESS 8 "Yes. The standard uniformitarian model requires many millions of years between layers. Such a long time should have produced enormous amounts of erosion."

ATTY CARDONA "What do you mean by uniformitarian?"

WITNESS 8 "Uniformitarian refers to the claim of Charles Lyell in the 1830s and his predecessor James Hutton in the 1780s that processes seen in the present are the same as those in the past. Most geologists continue to hold that view."

ATTY CARDONA "Was there a scientific basis for Hutton and Lyell's claim?"

WITNESS 8 "No. It was based on their religious views."

ATTY CARDONA "How do you know that?"

WITNESS 8 "In a lecture in 1832 at King's College London, Lyell expressed his view that 'the physical part of geological inquiry ought to be conducted as if the Scriptures were not in existence.' His private correspondence indicated that he was probably a Deist. The unpublished preface to Hutton's *The Theory of the Earth* indicated that he was also a Deist, or possibly an atheist."[80]

ATTY CARDONA "Please tell us what a Deist believes."

WITNESS 8 "Most Deists express the belief that there was a Creator, but that He does not interact with His creation. They specifically deny the existence of miracles. In the study of geology this belief is essentially the same as naturalism that denies a Creator completely."

ATTY CARDONA "Are there any other features of the earth that are flat today?"

WITNESS 8 "Yes. Forty percent of the earth's land surface is covered now by rather flat plateaus formed of sedimentary rock often several kilometers thick."

ATTY CARDONA "Are sedimentary rock deposits caused by flowing water?"

WITNESS 8 "Yes."

ATTY CARDONA "Could such plateaus be formed by many small floods over millions of years?"

WITNESS 8 "No. Living organisms typically disturb land surfaces within a few days after a flood, but no such disturbances are observed in the sediments of the plateaus."[81]

ATTY CARDONA "What is your conclusion about the formation of these plateaus?"

WITNESS 8 "The plateaus were formed by large-scale flooding events separated by at most a few days, consistent with runoff of the water near the end of Noah's flood."

ATTY CARDONA "What rates of erosion are observed today?"

WITNESS 8 "Rivers today erode the land in their basins at rates between one millimeter and about one meter per 1,000 years. The average is about 60 millimeters (about 2.36 in) per 1,000 years."[82]

ATTY CARDONA "How much erosion of the plateaus should be expected then in the time since Noah's flood?"

WITNESS 8 "Based mainly on genealogies in the Bible, flood geologists believe the flood occurred roughly 4,500 years ago. At the average of 60 millimeters of erosion per 1,000 years, we would expect only about 270 millimeters, or less than one foot of erosion."

ATTY CARDONA "What is your conclusion from that?"

WITNESS 8 "The existence of flat plateaus today is consistent with their formation around the time of Noah's flood."

Atty Cardona "What is the average height above sea level of the continents?"

Witness 8 "About 600 meters (about 2000 ft)."

Atty Cardona "How many years on average would it then take to erode the continents completely away?"

Witness 8 "About 600 meters divided by 60 millimeters per thousand years, or 10 million years."

Atty Cardona "Is that much less than in the uniformitarian model for the formation of the continents?"

Witness 8 "Yes. Evolutionary geologists speculate that the continents are about 2.5 billion years old on average."

Atty Cardona "Are there other examples of fast erosion?"

Witness 8 "Yes. Because of their steep slopes, mountains often exhibit erosion rates of one meter per 1,000 years, or 1,000 meters (over 3,000 feet) per million years. In 10 million years, even the highest mountains would disappear at that rate. Data taken for over a hundred years indicates that most beaches on the Hawaiian islands erode at a rate of about one-tenth of a meter per year, or 100 meters (over 300 feet) per thousand years."[83]

Atty Cardona "What is the explanation commonly given for formation of the rock arches in Arches National Park in Utah?"

Witness 8 "Millions of years of erosion and weathering are supposed to be responsible."

Atty Cardona "How many arches are in Arches National Park?"

Witness 8 "Over two thousand."

Atty Cardona "How many have collapsed recently?"

Witness 8 "According to park rangers, 43 collapsed between 1977 and 2015."

ATTY CARDONA "At that rate, how long would it take for all of them to collapse?"

WITNESS 8 "Only about 2000 years."[84]

ATTY CARDONA "What is your conclusion from that?"

WITNESS 8 "It wouldn't have taken millions of years for the arches to form, as commonly asserted."

ATTY CARDONA "No further questions of Witness 8. Your witness, Mr. Porter."

ATTY PORTER "Witness 8, you mentioned, did you not, that the canyons at Mount Saint Helens formed rapidly?"

WITNESS 8 "Yes."

ATTY PORTER "And you suggested that these canyons are like a miniature Grand Canyon, correct?"

WITNESS 8 "That is correct."

ATTY PORTER "The layers in the Grand Canyon are largely sandstone and limestone, correct?"

WITNESS 8 "Yes."

ATTY PORTER "How then can you compare those layers with the ash laid down by the Mount Saint Helens eruption?"

WITNESS 8 "Sediments of ash at the bottom of the picture I showed indeed exhibit no layering. However, the distinct sedimentary layers seen in the middle of the picture were deposited by flows of volcanic rock mixed with water and gas and moving at very high speeds, approximately 90 miles per hour. Similar conditions could have formed layers in the Grand Canyon during the Flood."

ATTY PORTER "Why aren't the walls of the canyons at Mount Saint Helens vertical like many of those in the Grand Canyon?"

WITNESS 8 "Some of the canyon walls at Mount Saint Helens are indeed quite vertical, such as the one shown in the picture I presented. Forming vertical walls requires hardening of the deposited material, and that also happened rapidly at Mount Saint Helens."

ATTY PORTER "You mentioned rapid erosion of mountains such as Mount Everest. It is true, is it not, that some uplifts occur presently at rates of up to ten meters per 1,000 years, which is more than the rate of erosion?"

WITNESS 8 "That is true in some locations."

ATTY PORTER "Is it not possible then that multiple uplifts in millions of years could counteract such erosion?"

WITNESS 8 "In any case, erosion in more than several thousand years would have destroyed the upper layers that contain the marine fossils that we see now near the top of Mount Everest."

ATTY PORTER "Please tell us what is the so-called 'water vapor canopy model.'"

WITNESS 8 "That was a model for supposed uniform temperatures around the Earth before the Flood and a partial source of the water in the Flood."

ATTY PORTER "Is it true that that model was proposed by creationists?"

WITNESS 8 "That is correct."

ATTY PORTER "What is the status of that model today?"

WITNESS 8 "Most creation scientists today have concluded the vapor canopy model is incorrect, for numerous Biblical and scientific reasons. I have already presented evidence for sources of water in the Flood."

ATTY PORTER "No further questions for Witness 8. I would like now to call Witness 9."

JUDGE JACOBSEN "Mr. Porter, let's take a short break before your next witness."

THE COURTROOM HALLWAY

Jason, Brian and Witness 8 walked down the hallway outside the courtroom and sat down on an isolated long bench near a window. Jason excitedly took some papers out of an envelope to show to the others.

"Get a load of this. Here's a picture taken of an arch called Darwin's arch near the Galápagos Islands that Darwin visited and made famous. And here's a picture of it right after it collapsed in 2021. It's just like all of Darwin's stuff—falling apart."[85]

Darwin's Arch Before   *Darwin's Arch After*

"That's truly ironic, isn't it?" Witness 8 remarked. "But much of the world hasn't gotten the message, especially those running our institutions. For example, The Grand Canyon National Park research office in 2014 refused to grant Dr. Snelling permission to collect some rock samples. A Freedom of Information Act request to the National Park Service yielded the comments by the three academic geologists who had reviewed his research application. All three had expressed scorn for his Christian faith and creationist worldview, insisting that his research not be permitted. Permission was given only after the Alliance Defending Freedom filed a lawsuit on Dr. Snelling's behalf. It was clearly a case of viewpoint discrimination."[86]

"Didn't you also tell me something similar about Dr. Neller?" Brian asked. "That when he started to think about how all the satellite pictures he'd seen suggested a worldwide flood, and he shared those feelings with colleagues, they counseled him to 'be logical' or else he would lose grant money?"

"That's right," Witness 8 confirmed, "and it's typical. Several fine Christians have lost their livelihoods that way."[87]

"Well, we'd better get back to the courtroom now," observed Brian, "and I expect we'll hear a flood of criticism."

Jason groaned a little and then smiled.

THE COURTROOM

GEOLOGY

The Geologic Strata: Continued

JUDGE JACOBSEN "The court is back in session."

ATTY PORTER "I would now like to call Witness 9, representing the work of Carol Hill, Dr. Gregg Davidson, Tim Helble and Wayne Ranney, editors of *Grand Canyon: Monument to an Ancient Earth*. Witness 9, please describe the background of these geologists."

WITNESS 9 "Carol Hill has been a geologist who worked in the Grand Canyon for over 17 years and was a specialist in caves. She received a master's degree in geology from the University of New Mexico. Dr. Davidson received his Ph.D. in hydrology from the University of Arizona and has served as the chair of the Geological Engineering Department at the University of Mississippi. Tim Helble has also been a hydrologist. He received a master's degree from the University of Arizona and worked for the National Weather Service. Wayne Ranney received a master's degree from Northern Arizona University and has been a geologist and trail guide."

ATTY PORTER "Where in the Grand Canyon is the Coconino sandstone layer?"

WITNESS 9 "Near the top."

ATTY PORTER "Does the evidence indicate how it was formed?"

WITNESS 9 "Yes. The evidence points to its formation by wind in a desert environment."

ATTY PORTER "Please describe for us some of that evidence."

WITNESS 9 "In deserts, wind causes dry sand to form sand dunes. When the sand becomes too steeply piled, it avalanches down the back side of the dune at a characteristic angle. Flowing wind then causes another dune to form, and the process is repeated. This process produces cross-bedding. Cross-beds in the Coconino sandstone have angles typical of desert dunes. Saturated sand in underwater dunes cannot maintain such a steep angle."[88]

ATTY PORTER "Is there other evidence for formation of the Coconino sandstone in a desert environment?"

WITNESS 9 "There are prints of raindrops in the sandstone. They could not occur if the sandstone sediment were under water or even in a rapidly rising flood environment."[89]

ATTY PORTER "What about footprints?"

WITNESS 9 "There many exquisite animal tracks, or footprints, preserved on surfaces of exposed cross-bedding in the Coconino sandstone. These tracks, and also burrows, resemble those made today in desert environments by spiders, scorpions and small reptiles. Tracks of vertebrates often occur in two rows as one would expect from four-legged animals."[90]

ATTY PORTER "How could such tracks be preserved?"

WITNESS 9 "Some moisture is required to form the tracks. Preservation of such tracks then generally requires hardening of the surface by evaporation of the moisture, leaving behind minerals that can hold the sand grains together."

ATTY PORTER "What would be the source of the moisture?"

WITNESS 9 "A good example is mist moving inland from an ocean, such as occurs today in the Namib desert in southwest Africa where tracks from small reptiles can be seen in the sand."[91]

ATTY PORTER "Why couldn't the Coconino tracks be formed in a flood environment?"

WITNESS 9 "Even slow flows of water would quickly wipe out any trace of footprints. Also, running and galloping gaits indicated in the Coconino sandstone are only possible on dry land."

ATTY PORTER "Let us turn now to the question of how the Grand Canyon was carved. Can you suggest the source of all the water to carve it out?"

WITNESS 9 "Yes. There are multiple streams at the east side of the Kaibab uplift, which is located on the east end of Grand Canyon."

ATTY PORTER "What is the Kaibab uplift?"

WITNESS 9 "It is a large plateau rising about 3,000 feet above the surrounding area."

ATTY PORTER "How could water rise up over this region in order to flow westward to make the Grand Canyon?"

WITNESS 9 "One suggestion derives from the observation that caves can easily form in limestone layers such as exist under the plateau. Streams could flow underground through these caves to the west side. When the caves later collapsed, a surface passage through the plateau would develop."[92]

ATTY PORTER "How do flood geologists explain the water flow?"

WITNESS 9 "They generally assume that there were very large prehistoric lakes, one called Hopi Lake, on the east side of the Kaibab plateau. When their natural dams were breached catastrophically, all the water in those lakes supposedly flowed out and carved the Grand Canyon."

ATTY PORTER "Is there evidence that anything like that ever occurred in the past?"

WITNESS 9 "Yes. Geologists generally agree that the Channeled Scablands in Washington State were formed by water flowing rapidly from one or several dam breaches at a large prehistoric lake called Lake Missoula."

ATTY PORTER "Could a similar event carve out the Grand Canyon?"

WITNESS 9 "No. First of all, while there is significant evidence for the existence of Lake Missoula, there is hardly any evidence for Hopi Lake or its partner. Secondly, the Channeled Scablands consist of many relatively shallow canyons that are not at all like the very deep single Grand Canyon."

ATTY PORTER "No further questions of Witness 9. Your witness, Mr. Cardona."

ATTY CARDONA "Witness 9, you mentioned that there is a characteristic angle of avalanching in desert sand dunes, correct?"

WITNESS 9 "Yes."

ATTY CARDONA "What is that characteristic angle?"

WITNESS 9 "About 30 degrees to 34 degrees."

ATTY CARDONA "What are the actual measured angles of cross-bedding in the Grand Canyon Coconino sandstone?"

WITNESS 9 "They are typical of desert dunes, with maximum angles of 29 to 31 degrees."

ATTY CARDONA "You also mentioned that the corresponding angle in underwater dunes is much less, correct?"

WITNESS 9 "Correct."

ATTY CARDONA "That is why you believe the Coconino sandstone was formed in a desert environment, correct?"

WITNESS 9 "That would be one reason."

ATTY CARDONA "Is it not true that the avalanching angle in underwater dunes formed by flowing water is roughly 20 degrees?"

WITNESS 9 "I suppose that is roughly correct."

ATTY CARDONA "I submit to you that creation geologists and others have measured the cross-bedding angle at over 200 locations of the Coconino sandstone and found an average angle of only about 20 degrees."[93]

WITNESS 9 "At some places it can be as high as 30 degrees."

ATTY CARDONA "But the angle at most places is more like 20 degrees?"

WITNESS 9 "I can't say."

ATTY CARDONA "You also mentioned that fossil prints looking like they were formed from raindrops on sand are seen in the Coconino sandstone, correct?"

"Please have a look at the photos that are shown in Exhibit 7. Does the photo on the left of this exhibit correctly show some of the prints that are considered to be from raindrops?"

WITNESS 9 "Yes."

ATTY CARDONA "Is it true that those prints are well-formed, looking like small craters?"

WITNESS 9 "You could say that in general, yes."

ATTY CARDONA "I will submit to you that the photo on the right side of this exhibit is a photo of the aftermath of rain falling on sand. Is it not true that rain drops falling on sand today produce a very mottled look as in this photo, with no evidence of individual drops?"

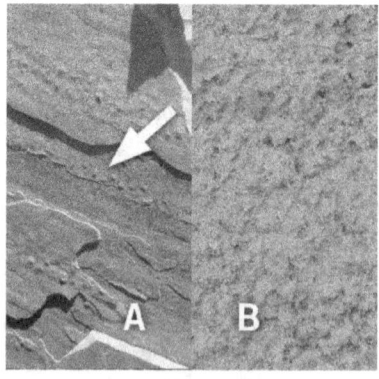

Exhibit 7. *A. Photo of prints allegedly formed by raindrops in Coconino sandstone.*
B. Photo of sand today after a rainfall.[94]

WITNESS 9 "Probably the Coconino prints were formed by a very light rain or mist."

ATTY CARDONA "Would such rain make well-formed craters in the sand?"

WITNESS 9 "I don't know."

ATTY CARDONA "You also mentioned that tracks of small animals in the Coconino sandstone are evidence of formation in desert environment, correct?"

WITNESS 9 "Correct."

ATTY CARDONA "Is it not true that those tracks are almost always observed on the slopes of the cross-bedding corresponding to the supposed original dunes?"

WITNESS 9 "That is your claim. I cannot say."

ATTY CARDONA "Is it also true that the toes in those tracks are often pointed in strange directions, not related to the animal's evident direction of travel?"

WITNESS 9 "That is seen in a few cases."

ATTY CARDONA "Would those track features not then be consistent with the animals climbing to escape rising floodwaters?"

WITNESS 9 "That is your interpretation."

ATTY CARDONA "Are you aware of laboratory studies of salamanders walking on various types of sand—dry, wet, and underwater, showing that the tracks that best matched the Coconino tracks were made underwater?"[95]

WITNESS 9 "Yes, but I understand those studies were done in very gently flowing water that was nothing like would have been seen in rising floodwaters."

ATTY CARDONA "Is it true that tracks in the Coconino sandstone often seem to begin and end suddenly?"

WITNESS 9 "In some cases."

ATTY CARDONA "Could flowing water explain the sudden appearance and disappearance of such tracks, as the currents picked up animals and dropped them in new places?"

WITNESS 9 "No."

ATTY CARDONA "Why is that? Why not?"

WITNESS 9 "I have already mentioned that rapidly flowing water would immediately destroy any footprints."

ATTY CARDONA "You mentioned that tracks must be hardened by expulsion of moisture in order for them to survive, correct?"

WITNESS 9 "Yes."

ATTY CARDONA "Is it not true that, in the flood model, floodwaters carry along large amounts of sediment as well as any animals?"

WITNESS 9 "Yes, that is their model."

ATTY CARDONA "Is it not reasonable that those sediments could have rapidly covered footprints of the animals and pressed out the water so that the footprints would be preserved?"

WITNESS 9 "That may be their model."

ATTY CARDONA "In discussing the origin of the water to carve out the Grand Canyon, you mentioned flow through underground caves at the Kaibab Plateau, correct?"

WITNESS 9 "Correct."

ATTY CARDONA "You also mentioned, did you not, that those caves were in limestone layers under the plateau?"

WITNESS 9 "Yes."

ATTY CARDONA "Is it not true that the bottom of those limestone layers is roughly 900 feet above the surrounding region?[96]"

WITNESS 9 "Yes."

ATTY CARDONA "How then could water flow from the east side up and over to the west side of the Kaibab plateau?"

WITNESS 9 "We are still working on a model. Science doesn't always have immediate answers. That is what science is about."

ATTY CARDONA "Are you aware of a flood model published over ten years ago suggesting that the Grand Canyon was carved by water runoff during the latter part of Noah's Flood when the waters were receding?"

WITNESS 9 "That would not solve the problem of getting over the Kaibab plateau."

ATTY CARDONA "It is true, is it not, that there are many so-called water gaps seen today where rivers seem to go through mountains rather than around them?"

WITNESS 9 "That is true."

ATTY CARDONA "It is generally agreed, is it not, that motion of the plates in the Earths' crust, called plate tectonics, was responsible for lifting up the Kaibab plateau?"

WITNESS 9 "Yes."

ATTY CARDONA "Are you familiar with the work of Dr. John Baumgardner showing how catastrophic plate tectonics could have been the driving force in the Flood?"[97,98]

WITNESS 9 "Yes, but his work has been contested by standard geologists. The heat generated by friction in such rapid motion of the plates would have boiled off most, if not all, of the Earth's oceans."[99]

ATTY CARDONA "I submit to you that glassy rock caused by high-speed frictional melting during superfaults is only about one foot thick.[100] Would that not indicate that the heat generated by such motion is vastly less than that required to boil oceans?"

WITNESS 9 "A detailed technical debate would be necessary to settle that issue."

ATTY CARDONA "Nevertheless, if catastrophic plate tectonics caused the uplift of the Kaibab plateau during the last phase of Noah's flood, could it not cause the water on top of the Kaibab plateau to run off westward and form the Grand Canyon, similar to the way water gaps are formed?"

WITNESS 9 "That might sound logical, but such water flowing over soft sediment that supposedly still existed during the Flood would not form the steep walls seen in the Canyon."

ATTY CARDONA "Why is that?"

WITNESS 9 "Formation of steep walls requires that the sediment first be hardened."

ATTY CARDONA "I submit that Witness 8 has already established that steep canyon walls formed rapidly in the mudflow not long after the main Mount Saint Helens eruption. No further questions, your honor."

JUDGE JACOBSEN "In that case, let us now break for lunch. Please be back on time so we can start promptly at 1:30. I understand we have a lot to cover this afternoon."

Brian turned to Jason and Witness 8 and remarked, "I guess we don't have time for a leisurely lunch. Let's just go to the courthouse cafeteria today. And I'd better eat with Witnesses 10, 11, and 12 to review notes for this afternoon."

"That's okay with me. Witness 8 and I can have lunch together," Jason suggested. Just then reporter Thomason walked over and asked Jason, "Can I join you for lunch?"

"Sure, come join us in the cafeteria."

THURSDAY NOON

THE COURTHOUSE CAFETERIA

As they were sitting down, Jason grabbed some hot sauce to go with his burritos and looked over at Mr. Thomason. "What have you got there?"

"Just some fish cakes with rice," Thomason replied.

"And I'm sticking with a little light chicken salad," Witness 8 said. "I need to unwind a bit from this morning."

A few minutes into their meal Witness 8 asked, "Jason, I understand that you had that book *Grand Canyon: Monument to an Ancient Earth* in your classroom library. That was the book Witness 9 testified about. Why did you do that?"

Jason explained. "Well, for one thing, it didn't seem to have nearly as much depth as some of the creation science books you testified about. So I thought it was a good comparison to creation science books. Also, only one of the four editors of that book had a Ph.D. The people you represented all had Ph.Ds. People are always complaining that creation science is fake science and creationists are uneducated fundamentalists, that sort of thing."

"You mean, like me?" Thomason chimed in half-teasingly.

"Sorry, Mr. Thomason, I didn't mean to offend you," Jason replied. "But I *have* been reading your online posts."

Witness 8 went on, "Did you know anything about the background to that book Witness 9 was drawing from?"

"Not much. I'm interested. What do you know?" Jason probed.

Witness 8 continued. "Well, funding for the book came from the ASA (that is, the American Scientific Affiliation), the John Templeton Foundation, and the BioLogos Foundation, all of which promote theistic evolution, including human evolution from ape-like creatures."[101]

"Wow," Jason said, "human evolution from ape-like creatures was being pushed at the so-called monkey trial, the Scopes trial, way back a hundred years ago. Nothing much has changed, I guess."

"Yes, and a lot of it was promoted by Christians just like now," Witness 8 added. "The defense in the Scopes Trial entered statements into the record from many noted scientists trying to show that there is no conflict between the Bible and evolution. Most of those scientists were professing Christians.

"After the *Monument to an Ancient Earth* book was published, its lead editor revealed in the journal of the ASA that the purpose of the book indeed was to make evolution acceptable.[102] The really sad part is that the book was endorsed by several well-known Christians, including some who have written against theistic biological evolution."

"Witness 8," Jason said, "I thought you needed to unwind a bit. You're still going strong, aren't you."

"Yeah, I'll just keep quiet now and enjoy my lunch."

Jason thought for a minute and then observed, "Yes, Christians really need to understand that geological evolution over millions of years is inseparable from some kind of biological evolution. If a Christian accepts millions of years for the formation of the geologic strata, he has to figure out where the fossils in those strata came from. Belief in a local flood instead of a worldwide flood doesn't get around that problem, since there are fossils all over the world. If he rejects gradual 'theistic' evolution with God tacked on, his only explanation then would be that God created all the creatures in bursts separated by tens or hundreds of millions of years. That's just like the 'punctuated equilibrium' idea promoted by evolutionist Stephen J Gould, but with God tacked on again."

Jason went on, "And that makes God the overseer, if not the originator, of death, violence, disease, and suffering, all of which are part of the fossil record. He would be a very inefficient Creator at that. On the contrary, we know from Genesis 1 that God created everything very good at the beginning. From First Corinthians 15 we also know that death is an enemy, the last enemy that will be destroyed. Death and evil in the world came through the disobedience of Adam and Eve."

Thomason observed, "Very interesting. I never heard all this before."

"Meanwhile," Jason concluded, "Let's clean up and put back our trays. We don't have a million years to get back to the courtroom."

THURSDAY AFTERNOON

THE COURTROOM

GEOLOGY

Radioactive Decay Dating: Carbon 14

JUDGE JACOBSEN "Are we all ready? Okay, the court is back in session. Mr. Cardona, go ahead with your witness."

ATTY CARDONA "Now I would like to call Witness 10, representing the work of Dr. John Baumgardner on radioactive decay dating using carbon 14. Witness 10, what is the background of Dr. Baumgardner?"

WITNESS 10 "Dr. Baumgardner received a Ph.D. in geophysics from UCLA. He worked for several years at the Los Alamos National Laboratory, where he developed large computer programs. One such program was a model for catastrophic plate tectonics that could explain motion of the earth's crust during the Flood of Noah's time. Later he worked with other Ph.D. creation scientists in the RATE project dealing with radioactive decay dating."

ATTY CARDONA "Please tell us, what is the main feature of carbon 14 dating?"

WITNESS 10 "Carbon 14 is very useful in determining the age of relatively young objects that contain carbon."

ATTY CARDONA "Why is that?"

WITNESS 10 "Carbon 14 decays rapidly compared to other radioactive elements."

ATTY CARDONA "What does the 14 in carbon 14 stand for?"

WITNESS 10 "The nuclei at the center of carbon atoms have protons and neutrons. The total number of those is the atomic weight, in this case 14. Carbon 14 has six protons and eight neutrons, while stable carbon 12 has six protons and six neutrons. The number of electrons in a single atom is the same as the number of protons and determines its chemical behavior. All forms of carbon have six protons and six electrons and hence behave the same chemically."

ATTY CARDONA "Can you explain how carbon 14 is generated?"

WITNESS 10 "First of all, high energy particles called cosmic rays are continually impinging on the earth's upper atmosphere. A large fraction of these particles is charged helium nuclei known as alpha particles. Collisions of these particles with other particles in the upper atmosphere release neutrons. Those neutrons in turn collide with nitrogen in the atmosphere and transform it to radioactive carbon 14."

ATTY CARDONA "What happens then?"

WITNESS 10 "Carbon 14 combines with oxygen in the atmosphere to form CO_2, carbon dioxide. Most carbon dioxide contains carbon 12, but some contains this radioactive carbon 14. Living plants then ingest both forms of carbon dioxide during photosynthesis. Carbon 14 decays into nitrogen with a half-life of 5,730 years. When plant material dies, it ceases to ingest carbon from the atmosphere, but the carbon 14 left in it continues to decay. By measuring the ratio of the remaining carbon 14 to carbon 12 in the material today, we can estimate how old the plant material was when it died. Animals also ingest living plant material and so contain similar amounts of carbon 14 when they are fossilized."

ATTY CARDONA "What is the meaning of 'half-life?'"

WITNESS 10 "The half-life of a radioactive element is the time it takes for half of it to decay. After two half-lives, one-quarter remains, after three half-lives one-eighth, and so on. After ten half-lives, only about 0.1 percent, or one-thousandth, remains. In the case of carbon 14, ten half-lives is ten times 5,730 years, or 57,300 years."

ATTY CARDONA "What is the maximum age that can be determined now by carbon 14 decay?"

WITNESS 10 "AMS techniques developed in the late 1970s can detect carbon 14 to carbon 12 ratios corresponding to ages up to about 80,000 years."

ATTY CARDONA "What does AMS stand for?"

WITNESS 10 "Accelerator mass spectrometer."

ATTY CARDONA "Can contamination by random carbon present in an AMS laboratory affect the dating results?"

WITNESS 10 "Yes. The samples used in AMS dating are small, so much care is taken to avoid contaminating them."

ATTY CARDONA "How does one know that contamination is not present?"

WITNESS 10 "An AMS lab typically will prepare a 'calibration' blank of some material that is thought to contain no carbon 14, such as Precambrian graphite or a calcium carbonate mineral called calcite. If the standard process then detects any carbon 14 from the calibration blank, it is assumed that it came from the background environment and it subtracted from the amount of C14 measured in the sample of interest."[103]

ATTY CARDONA "Why do the labs assume the materials used for the calibration have no carbon 14?"

WITNESS 10 "Mainstream geologists assume they are millions or billions of years old and should therefore contain no measurable C14."

ATTY CARDONA "Is that accurate?"

WITNESS 10 "We expect that it may not be."

ATTY CARDONA "What then is the effect on the measured dates of the standard practice of subtracting the amount of C14 assumed to be background C14 from the total C14 measured in the sample of interest?"

WITNESS 10 "It would increase the measured age. So we expect that the laboratory results of measurements on our samples are their maximum ages."

ATTY CARDONA "What materials were investigated by Dr. Baumgardner and his group?"

WITNESS 10 "Ten samples of coal were obtained from the US Department of Energy Coal Sample Bank, maintained by Pennsylvania State University."

ATTY CARDONA "Coal is formed from plant material, correct?"

WITNESS 10 "Yes."

ATTY CARDONA "What are the conventional ages of the samples?"

WITNESS 10 "The samples were from three different geologic strata with conventional ages of about 300, 100, and 45 million years, respectively."

ATTY CARDONA "What were the measured results?"

WITNESS 10 "The average measured carbon 14 to carbon 12 ratio was about 0.25 percent of the ratio in the present-day atmosphere, after about 0.08 percent of supposed 'background' C14 was subtracted. The measured ratios varied from about 0.1 percent to 0.46 percent, but the average was about the same for samples from all three geologic strata."[104]

ATTY CARDONA "What is the age for these samples corresponding to the measured C14/C12 ratios?"

WITNESS 10 "A ratio of 0.25 percent corresponds to the decay in 8.6 half-lives, or 49,500 years. The total measured range of 0.1 percent to 0.46 percent corresponds to ages ranging from about 44,500 to 57,000 years."

ATTY CARDONA "What is your conclusion from these results?"

Witness 10 "The results are consistent with recent almost simultaneous deposition of the coal in all of the geologic strata, such as would be expected during a recent worldwide flood lasting one year."

Atty Cardona "Have other people published similar results?"

Witness 10 "An examination of articles in standard journals revealed roughly a hundred cases where significant amounts of carbon 14 were measured, not only in coal but also in oil, fossils, petrified wood and inorganic calcite."[105]

Atty Cardona "What were the standard explanations for the observed carbon 14?"

Witness 10 "The observed C14 was generally not understood, since it is commonly believed that the materials were too old to contain any measurable C14."

Atty Cardona "Did Dr. Baumgardner's group investigate samples of other materials?"

Witness 10 "Yes."

Atty Cardona "What were those?"

Witness 10 "Twelve samples of diamonds from West and South Africa were sent to one the foremost AMS labs in the world."

Atty Cardona "Do diamonds contain carbon?"

Witness 10 "Diamond is the hardest form of pure carbon."

Atty Cardona "What were the results?"

Witness 10 "The measured ratio of C14 to C12 in these samples varied from 0.02 percent to 0.31 percent of the ratio in today's atmosphere, even after 0.08 percent of supposed 'background' was subtracted. The corresponding ages vary from about 48,000 to 70,000 years."[106]

Atty Cardona "Why is this result significant?"

WITNESS 10 "Inclusions sometimes found in diamonds give conventional ages of up to billions of years. The carbon 14 results evidently invalidate those conventional dating methods."

ATTY CARDONA "No further questions. Your witness, Mr. Porter."

ATTY PORTER "Is it not possible that the carbon 14 measured in coal samples came recently into the coal from the atmosphere or from groundwater long after the coal was deposited?"

WITNESS 10 "The samples came from coal seams with much different thicknesses and porosities and at much different depths in the geologic column. If your explanation were true, the samples should therefore have exhibited vastly different ratios of carbon 14 to carbon 12, but the measured ratios were roughly the same. In addition, diamond is more resistant to interaction with the environment than any other material. It is the hardest known material and has an extremely high melting point. Hence no carbon 14 could enter diamond after its formation. Nevertheless, the diamond samples measured by Dr. Baumgardner contained significant amounts of C14."[107]

ATTY PORTER "Could not neutrons from the environment enter the samples and generate carbon 14?"

WITNESS 10 "That is possible. However, calculations indicate that the amount of C14 that could be produced that way is several thousand times less than what was observed."[108]

ATTY PORTER "Is it not true that creationists assume that a worldwide flood occurred about 4,500 years ago?"

WITNESS 10 "Yes."

ATTY PORTER "But the coal sample data indicated ages of roughly 50,000 years, correct?"

WITNESS 10 "Correct."

ATTY PORTER "How then could the carbon 14 measurements on those samples be consistent with the supposed worldwide flood?"

WITNESS 10 "There are several reasons, all having to do with a lower ratio of C14 to C12 existing in plants living before the flood than today. Since the ages deduced from the AMS measurements all assume that the C14/C12 ratio in living plants has remained unchanged, those deduced ages can be much longer than the actual ages.

"First of all, the flood buried an enormous amount of plant and animal material. Hence there was much more total carbon 12 in plant material living before the flood than today. If the amount of carbon 14 in the atmosphere were the same before the flood as today, then the ratio of carbon 14 to carbon 12 in plant material living before the flood would be much less than it is today.

"Secondly, the amount of carbon 14 in the atmosphere today is probably much less than it was before the flood. One reason is that carbon 14 in the atmosphere today still has not reached equilibrium. More C14 is being produced in the atmosphere now than is leaving. That suggests that no C14 existed in the atmosphere at the time of creation only a few thousand years ago."[109]

"Also, there is substantial evidence that the earth's magnetic field is decreasing rapidly and would have been much greater before the flood. I understand that another witness at this trial will provide such evidence. The magnetic field shields the earth from incoming cosmic radiation and therefore cosmic radiation would have produced less carbon 14 in the atmosphere before the flood."[110]

ATTY PORTER "No further questions for Witness 10."

GEOLOGY

Radioactive Decay Dating: Uranium and Helium

ATTY CARDONA "Now I would like to call witness Witness 11, representing the work of Dr. Russell Humphreys. Witness 11, please summarize his background."

WITNESS 11 "Dr. Humphreys received a bachelor's degree in physics from Duke University and a Ph.D. in physics from Louisiana State University. He worked for several years at the high voltage laboratory of General Electric and then at Sandia National Laboratories in nuclear physics, geophysics, pulsed-power research, and theoretical atomic and nuclear physics."

ATTY CARDONA "Please describe the setting of the research on radioactive decay dating done by Dr. Humphreys."

WITNESS 11 "Los Alamos National Laboratory in New Mexico, in 1974, had been interested in whether heat trapped underground could be used as a source of energy called geothermal energy. The laboratory bored a hole 4.3 kilometers deep in nearby granite down to Precambrian strata. They labeled the samples obtained from the hole with the temperature at the depth they were taken. Black mica called biotite was extracted from the granite in each sample, and then small crystals of zirconium silicate called zircons were extracted from the biotite."[111]

ATTY CARDONA "Why were the zircons of special interest?"

WITNESS 11 "Radioactive decay dating of rocks depends on at least three assumptions. Two of these are satisfied exceptionally well in zircons."

ATTY CARDONA "What are those two assumptions?"

WITNESS 11 "First of all, the amount of the final decay product, or daughter atom, has to be known at the time when the decay started. That time is usually assumed to be the time when the rock first cooled. Secondly, there has to be no interaction of the rock with its environment that could cause the parent, any intermediate decay product, or the final decay product, to leak in or out of the rock. Uranium, for example, can move in or out of some rocks through groundwater."

ATTY CARDONA "How are those assumptions satisfied in zircons?"

WITNESS 11 "Firstly, when zircons cool down from some volcanic activity in Precambrian strata, they can easily incorporate some uranium as they crystallize. Due to the similar chemical behavior of uranium and zirconium, up to four percent of the zirconium atoms can be replaced by uranium during this process. By far the largest concentration of uranium in the earth is U238, with atomic weight 238. Its final decay product is lead with atomic weight 206 or lead 206. That form, or isotope, of lead, only results from the decay of U238. Because the chemical behavior of lead is much different from that of zirconium, no lead can be incorporated into zircons during cool down. Hence, we know there was zero lead 206 at the start of the decay of U238.

"Secondly, lead 206 cannot get out of solid zircon once it is formed. One intermediate decay product produced on the way between U238 and lead 206 is radon gas. Nevertheless, radon is a heavy atom and decays with a four-day half-life, so it does not significantly leak out of a zircon crystal."

ATTY CARDONA "What is the third assumption in radioactive decay dating?"

WITNESS 11 "The third assumption is that the rates of decay are constant."

Atty Cardona "Why was that assumption suspect for the samples taken by Los Alamos National Laboratory?"

Witness 11 "In 1982, a physicist named Dr. Robert Gentry of Oak Ridge National Laboratory measured and published the concentration of helium in zircons from all the samples. The original temperature of six samples when removed from the borehole was between about 100 degrees Celsius and 300 degrees.

"The helium concentration, or number of helium atoms per unit volume of zircon, was unexpectedly large. Helium is formed in zircons as a byproduct of the individual decay steps in the uranium decay process. That process generates alpha particles, which are positively charged helium nuclei. Those nuclei capture electrons in the zircon crystal and form helium atoms. Helium is a very light gas and should escape relatively easily from zircons."[112]

Atty Cardona "What did Dr. Humphreys and his group do then?"

Witness 11 "First of all, some zircons from one of the Los Alamos lab's borehole samples were sent to a standard dating lab. The 1439-million-year date determined by that lab was close to an earlier published result of 1500 million years."

Atty Cardona "How is that age determined?"

Witness 11 "The concentrations of uranium 238 and lead 206 in the zircon are measured. Those concentrations are the number of those atoms per unit volume of zircon. From the present known decay rate of uranium 238 and the relative concentrations of those atoms, the age is calculated. There are many other decays of atoms on the way from uranium 238 to lead 206 such as thorium, radium, radon, polonium and bismuth, but the total time for those other intermediate decays is less than 0.01 percent of the time for the initial decay of uranium 238 to thorium 234. Lead 206 is stable and does not decay."

Atty Cardona "What else can be determined from those measurements?"

WITNESS 11 "Each decay from one uranium 238 atom to one lead 206 atom generates a total of eight helium atoms through all the intermediate decay steps. So the concentration of helium should be eight times the measured concentration of lead 206, assuming that no helium leaked out of the zircon."

ATTY CARDONA "Can the age of zircons be checked then by measuring the concentration of helium in them?"

WITNESS 11 "If the leakage rate of helium, that is, its diffusivity, is known, then one can also calculate the age of the zircon by comparing its present concentration of helium with the measured concentration of lead 206."

ATTY CARDONA "How was the diffusivity of helium from the zircons measured?"

WITNESS 11 "Over one thousand tiny zircons separated from one of the rock samples were sent to an independent laboratory through a third party. That lab measured the diffusivity at about 20 different temperatures, from 171 degrees Celsius to 550 degrees.

"At the highest temperature the diffusivity, or rate of leakage, was almost a million times greater than at the lowest temperature."[113]

ATTY CARDONA "What were the calculated ages of the zircon samples then?"

WITNESS 11 "For all three of the six samples whose original temperatures overlapped with the temperatures of the diffusivity measurements, the calculated ages were very close to 6,000 years. The diffusivity measurements could be extrapolated down to about 100 degrees Celsius, and again a 6,000 plus-minus 2,000-year age was calculated for all three samples at original temperatures between about 100 and 150 degrees Celsius."[114]

ATTY CARDONA "What were the conclusions then?"

WITNESS 11 "The age of the zircons is consistent with a recent creation. The uranium originally in them decayed in about 6,000 years, not 1.5 billion years. Somehow the decay rate of uranium has changed in the recent past."

ATTY CARDONA "No further questions. Your witness, Mr. Porter."

ATTY PORTER "You indicated that the zircon crystals are surrounded by biotite, correct?"

WITNESS 11 "Yes."

ATTY PORTER "Could the biotite not trap the helium from escaping?"

WITNESS 11 "No, for three reasons. Firstly, the diffusivity of helium in biotite is much higher than in zircons, so helium can readily escape through biotite. Secondly, calculations indicate that there is no barrier to helium leakage at the boundary between zircons and biotite. Finally, zircons are sandwiched between flat biotite mica layers, so helium has an exit path at the end of the biotite layers."[115]

ATTY PORTER "Is it not true that radioactive decay causes defects in zircons that can let helium leak out more rapidly?"

WITNESS 11 "That is true, but the effect is only about a factor of two in diffusivity. That is within the estimated precision of the measurements."

ATTY PORTER "Is it not possible that helium leaked into the zircons from outside and therefore made it appear that less had leaked out?"

WITNESS 11 "No. The concentration of helium in a biotite sample was more than 200 times less than the helium concentration in the embedded zircon."[116]

ATTY PORTER "You have indicated, have you not, that the helium leak rate, or diffusivity, decreases rapidly as the temperature is decreased?"

WITNESS 11 "Yes."

ATTY PORTER "Could not the samples have been much cooler in the past, thus reducing the amount of helium that escaped?"

WITNESS 11 "No. Analysis by the Los Alamos National Laboratory indicates that, in fact, the location of the borehole from which the samples were taken was likely much hotter in the past due to volcanic activity nearby."

ATTY PORTER "Is it not true that radioactive decay generates heat?"

WITNESS 11 "Yes."

ATTY PORTER "And some spacecraft are actually powered by such heat?"

WITNESS 11 "Yes, although in such cases the half-life of the radioactive material is typically only about a hundred years."

ATTY PORTER "Why wouldn't a vastly increased decay rate such as you claim existed in the zircon crystals have produced so much heat that it would have melted them?"

WITNESS 11 "Dr. Humphreys has proposed an interesting model for the heat removal based on clues from the Bible and modern physics. For one thing, it is known that what we call space is not empty. Physicists call it the quantum vacuum, for example. It has mass, oscillates like particles, and determines the speed of light.

"We can all move through it somewhat like free electrons move through solid conductors. The Bible also states that what it calls the heavens can be stretched out, torn, rolled up and split apart.[117] It compares the heavens to a fabric. Hence there seems to be some hyperspace perpendicular to that fabric.

"At the time of Noah's flood, the Bible states that the windows of the heavens were opened. Dr. Humphreys suggested that at that time, infrared radiation could pass through those windows into hyperspace. Materials radiate heat from their bodies in the form of infrared radiation, and that heat is proportional to the fourth power of their absolute temperature. Hence hot materials radiate much more than cool ones. Sources of radioactive decay could then cool much more than humans, for example, that were near room temperature. The accelerated nuclear decay would cease at the end of the Flood."[118]

ATTY PORTER "No further questions now for Witness 11."

Judge Jacobsen "All right, we'd better take another 15-minute break now before the next witness."

A SHORT BREAK

Outside the courtroom, Brian, Jason, and Witnesses 10, 11 and 12 circled up to chat. Turning to the Witnesses, Brian remarked, "It's really impressive what the seven scientists including Baumgardner, Humphreys and Snelling accomplished in seven years in the RATE project. Remind me when that was."

"It was from 1997 to 2004," Witness 12 replied, "and then it was all summarized in the book *Thousands...not Billions* published in 2005."

"Why do you think it's been this long and yet Christians, especially intellectuals, generally still don't know about it?" Jason asked.

"I suppose that's at least partly because few colleges or seminaries consider it, and the professors who do know about it are influenced by peer pressure," Witness12 observed.

"How is that going to change?" Brian wondered. "I guess, for now, we'd better do the best we can today."

GEOLOGY

Radioactive Decay Dating: Rocks

ATTY CARDONA "My next witness is Witness 12, representing the work of Dr. Andrew Snelling. Witness 8 already described his background. Witness 12, please tell us about some of the rocks analyzed by Dr. Snelling."

WITNESS 12 "Dr. Snelling and his group collected a total of over one-hundred rock samples from ten locations well studied by geologists, including five locations in the Grand Canyon, two elsewhere in Arizona, and one each in Wyoming, Australia and New Zealand. At each location the samples were carefully chosen to be representative of the region."

ATTY CARDONA "How were the rocks prepared?"

WITNESS 12 "The exteriors were removed to avoid possible contamination. The interiors of the samples were washed, dried, crushed to power and sorted by particle size. They were then sent to several laboratories for dating."[119]

ATTY CARDONA "What dating methods were used by those laboratories?"

WITNESS 12 "Four standard radioactive decay series were used, including lead-lead [Pb-Pb], samarium to neodymium [Sm-Nd], rubidium to strontium [Rb-Sr] and potassium to argon [K-Ar]. In the case of lead-lead dating, one compares the concentrations of the two different lead isotopes generated by the two radioactive uranium parent atoms U-238 and U-235, and sometimes the lead isotope generated by thorium decay. The known present decay rates of the radioactive parent atoms were used to calculate the ages."

Atty Cardona "Were any techniques used to eliminate uncertainty in the initial concentrations of the daughter atoms?"

Witness 12 "Yes. For each decay series, several samples from the same rock formation were measured and the so-called isochron method was used to estimate the age. In principle, this method eliminates uncertainty in the initial daughter concentrations. However, the statistical uncertainties of the quoted results are often very large, even more than plus and minus 50 percent."

Atty Cardona "Are there any instances when the isochron method gives incorrect results?"

Witness 12 "Sometimes there is too much scatter in the data to obtain an age. Other times an isochron age is determined with very good precision, but the age can be incorrect. That can happen, for example, if hot volcanic magma inherited daughter atoms from source rocks deep below the surface before rising into a volcanic eruption at the earth's surface. Then the measured age is much older than the age of the eruption."[120]

Atty Cardona "That is an example where the first assumption of radioactive decay dating is violated, correct?"

Witness 12 "Yes. Radioactive decay dating requires that the initial concentration of the daughter atoms be known or can be determined."

Atty Cardona "What are other situations where that assumption is violated, namely when daughter or parent atoms leak in or out of magma before it participates in a volcanic eruption?"

Witness 12 "Magma may melt some of the surrounding rocks on its way up to the earth's surface and incorporate some atoms from those rocks. Underground heated water and gaseous fluids seeping through fissures or pores in the surrounding rock can also introduce parent or daughter atoms into the magma."[121]

Atty Cardona "What were some of the results of the ages determined for the samples investigated by Dr. Snelling?"

WITNESS 12 "One region of special interest is Mt. Ngauruhoe in New Zealand. This active volcano was called 'Mt. Doom' in the *Lord of the Rings* movie trilogy. Samples of rocks from lava flows known to be less than one-hundred years old yielded isochron ages of approximately 133 million years, 197 million years and almost 4 billion years by the rubidium-strontium, samarium-neodymium and lead-lead methods, respectively. The test laboratory attached a statistical uncertainty of roughly ten percent to the lead-lead results, but much larger uncertainties for the other two results."[122]

ATTY CARDONA "Did some other results contradict ages that have supposedly been well established previously?"

WITNESS 12 "Yes. Samples taken from lava that flowed over the rim of the Grand Canyon at the Uinkaret Plateau yielded ages of roughly one billion years. The statistical uncertainties of these isochron data from the rubidium-strontium and samarium-neodymium methods were about 20 percent and 60 percent, respectively. One billion years is much longer than the age of about one million years for these lava flows cited in conventional publications. One billion years is even older than the conventional ages for many of the Grand Canyon strata over which the lava flowed."[123]

ATTY CARDONA "Are there examples of ages that individually seem very precise but are obviously not correct?"

WITNESS 12 "Yes. Dr. Snelling's group sent out for testing samples of Precambrian metamorphic rock called Brahma amphibolite taken from near the bottom of the Grand Canyon. About twenty samples were used to generate isochron ages for each of the rubidium-strontium, samarium-neodymium and lead-lead methods, and then another lot of about twenty samples for each method was used to generate another set of ages.

"The statistical uncertainties were only about 4 percent or less for the samarium-neodymium and lead-lead results, and 7 percent to 10 percent for the rubidium-strontium results. The results were repeatable for the two sets of samarium-neodymium and lead-lead results, yielding isochron ages of about 1.67 and 1.87 billion years, respectively. The isochron ages obtained for the two sets of rubidium-strontium tests were about 0.84 and 1.24 billion years, respectively. Clearly, all these results differed from each other by much more the statistical uncertainties cited by the test laboratory."[124]

ATTY CARDONA "What conclusions can you make from all these data?"

WITNESS 12 "Radioactive decay dating of rocks is unreliable due to violations of one or more of the three assumptions made in the dating. The concentration of daughter atoms at time zero may not be determinable, there may be leakage of parent and daughter atoms in and out of the rocks, and thirdly the rate of decay may not have been constant."

ATTY CARDONA "A non-constant rate of decay was already mentioned by Witness 11 in the case of uranium decay, was it not?"

WITNESS 12 "Yes, that is correct."

ATTY CARDONA "No further questions. Your witness, Mr. Porter."

ATTY PORTER "In lieu of questions for Witness 12, I would like to call witness Witness 13, representing the work of Dr. Roger Wiens. Witness 13, please tell us a little bit about the background of Dr. Wiens."

WITNESS 13 "Dr. Wiens received a Ph.D. in physics with a minor in geology from the University of Minnesota. He has worked at Caltech and Los Alamos National Laboratory, where he has been the leader of two projects using laser instrumentation on Mars rovers. He published a well-received online book titled *Radiometric Dating: A Christian Perspective*."

ATTY PORTER "What is the generally accepted age of the Earth?"

WITNESS 13 "About 4.5 billion years."

ATTY PORTER "How do we know that?"

WITNESS 13 "A geochemist named Clare Patterson first determined that age from radioactive decay measurements on meteorites in 1956. Since then, rocks from the Moon have yielded ages up to almost 4.5 billion years also."

ATTY PORTER "Are ages of rocks on the Earth similarly old?"

WITNESS 13 "Active processes on the Earth continue to break down and create rocks, so Earth rocks are not quite as old. Nevertheless, some rocks have been dated to between three and four billion years old."

ATTY PORTER "What about rocks in the Grand Canyon?"

WITNESS 13 "Some lava flows from the thick Cardenas layer in Precambrian strata exhibit an age of about 1.1 billion years."[125]

ATTY PORTER "What is metamorphism?"

WITNESS 13 "If volcanic rock subsequently gets hot, but not hot enough to completely re-melt the rock, the characteristics of the rock can change. Such change is called metamorphism. Some of the melted part of the rock will be mixed with the part that didn't melt."

ATTY PORTER "Why is that important?"

WITNESS 13 "An age cannot be determined for the rock in many such cases."

ATTY PORTER "Is an example of that the Brahma amphibolite mentioned by Witness 12?"

WITNESS 13 "Yes."

ATTY PORTER "What significance does that have?"

WITNESS 13 "Measured dates for those rocks are expected to be meaningless."

ATTY PORTER "Are there other cases where dates could be expected to be meaningless?"

WITNESS 13 "Yes, a 300,000-year date for the recent lava flows at Mount Saint Helens is commonly cited by flood geologists as evidence for the unreliability of radioactive dating."

ATTY PORTER "What is the problem with that date?"

WITNESS 13 "For one thing, older rock fragments no doubt mixed with the magma as it was coming to the surface of the volcano and then flowing out. Secondly, the potassium-argon method was used to obtain the age. Processes working in the environment are known to affect that method when used on rocks from lava flows. A more reliable method is the argon-argon method, which has successfully been used to date Mount Vesuvius, for example."[126]

ATTY PORTER "Is there an example where radioactive decay dating was used successfully to test a hypothesis in the present?"

WITNESS 13 "Yes. Continents are known to be slowly spreading apart at present. For example, Africa and North America are spreading apart from the mid-Atlantic ridge. Lava is continually welling up at this ridge and causing expansion of the Earth's crust at the ocean floor. Radioactive decay measurements of the crust at the edges of the continents yielded a maximum age of about 180 million years."[127]

ATTY PORTER "What is the significance of that age?"

WITNESS 13 "From the present distance of 3,480 miles between North America and northwest Africa and the measured age of 180 million years, we can calculate that the continents must have been spreading apart at an average rate of about 1.2 inches per year. That is in remarkable agreement with recent satellite station measurements."

ATTY PORTER "No further questions. Your witness, Mr. Cardona."

ATTY CARDONA "Witness 13, why were meteorite samples considered suitable for dating the age of the Earth?"

WITNESS 13 "It is generally assumed that meteorites are left over from a contracting nebula that also formed the Earth."

ATTY CARDONA "That is the so-called nebular hypothesis of Laplace, is it not?"

WITNESS 13 "Yes."

ATTY CARDONA "How do we know that hypothesis is true?"

WITNESS 13 "That is the standard model used by cosmologists."

ATTY CARDONA "You mentioned, did you not, that ages determined for metamorphic rocks such as the Brahma Amphibolite rocks cited by Witness 12 could be expected to be meaningless?"

WITNESS 13 "Yes."

ATTY CARDONA "Is that because the ages determined by the rubidium-strontium decay method exhibited a large variation from 0.84 to 1.24 billion years?"

WITNESS 13 "That would be one reason."

ATTY CARDONA "Is it not also true that Witness 12 cited ages with very low statistical uncertainty obtained for the same rocks by the samarium-neodymium and lead-lead methods?"

WITNESS 13 "Yes."

ATTY CARDONA "Why then would you not trust those latter two measurements to give valid ages?"

WITNESS 13 "As I said before, metamorphic rocks often do not give reliable ages."

ATTY CARDONA "How do you know that?"

WITNESS 13 "I mentioned mixing of partially melted and unmelted rocks."

ATTY CARDONA "Would your conclusion not also partly be because the latter two ages differed from each other by much more than the statistical uncertainties quoted by the measurement lab?"

WITNESS 13 "That could be part of the reason."

ATTY CARDONA "Were the rock samples from the Cardenas lava flow that you mentioned affected by metamorphism?"

WITNESS 13 "No."

ATTY CARDONA "So the 1.1-billion-year age that you cited for those rocks should be trustworthy, correct?"

WITNESS 13 "Correct."

ATTY CARDONA "I will submit to you that over twenty rocks taken by Dr. Snelling's group from the Cardenas lava flow yielded ages from 892, plus-minus 82 million years by the rubidium-strontium method to 1,588, plus-minus 170 million years by the samarium-neodymium method. How then can you claim that a 1.1-billion-year age for this lava flow is trustworthy?"

WITNESS 13 "I would have to look over the data that you cited."

ATTY CARDONA "You mentioned that radioactive decay dating yielded an age for the Earth's crust near the continental edges of about 180 million years, correct?"

WITNESS 13 "Yes."

ATTY CARDONA "Are you aware of publications indicating that the age of the crust near the edge of the continents is closer to 120 million years than 180 million years?"

WITNESS 13 "I only stated that maximum ages of about 180 million years were obtained."

ATTY CARDONA "You also stated that new crust is currently being generated at the mid-Atlantic ridge, correct?"

WITNESS 13 "Correct."

ATTY CARDONA "So the age of the current mid-Atlantic crust zero, is it not?"

WITNESS 13 "That is true."

ATTY CARDONA "And you assume, do you not, that current processes have continued to push the continents apart at an average rate of about an inch per year for the past 180 million years?"

WITNESS 13 "Yes."

ATTY CARDONA "That also means that the age of the crust must be proportional to its distance from the mid-Atlantic ridge, correct?"

WITNESS 13 "That would be so."

ATTY CARDONA "I submit to you that a further publication reported an age of 140 million years for the age of some rocks near the mid-Atlantic ridge.[128] Is that not an indication that these ages for the rocks are unreliable?"

WITNESS 13 "I would have to examine their work carefully."

ATTY CARDONA "No further questions."

JUDGE JACOBSEN "If there are no further witnesses on this topic, the court will now adjourn until tomorrow morning."

THURSDAY EVENING

THE RADCLIFFE FAMILY KITCHEN

Jason walked in the front door and over to the kitchen where Carol was making supper. Collin was sitting at the table looking at a dinosaur book. After a brief kiss, Jason said to Carol, "Did you know that you are radioactive?"

"Well, I know that you love me and find me attractive, but why am I 'radioactive?'" Carol laughed.

"That's because all the vegetables you eat contain some radioactive carbon 14 they got from carbon dioxide in the air. Not only that, but the granite countertop you are working on is probably radioactive."

"Oh, you can't be serious, dear. You must still be giddy from the testimonies today."

"No, I really am serious. Do you see those black shapes here and there in the granite? That's called biotite mica. And inside the biotite are so-called zircons that typically contain some radioactive uranium."

"Should I be worried?" Carol asked.

"Fortunately, no. Any uranium now would take billions of years to give off much radiation."

"You say, 'now.' Was it ever different?"

"Yes, probably at the time of Noah's Flood the decay was much faster."

"Wouldn't that much radiation have killed Noah and his family?"

"The immense quantity of water under the Ark might have protected them, just as the water in a nuclear reactor."

At the mention of Noah's Ark, Collin lifted his head up from the book. "Daddy," he asked, "how did Noah fit all the dinosaurs into the Ark? How did he even get them in the door?"

"Well, first of all, you are looking at pictures of grown-up dinosaurs. Noah didn't have to take grown-ups; God could have sent him little boy and girl dinosaurs."

"Oh?" Collin squinted his eyes as though thinking hard.

"Besides that," Jason continued, "even most grown-up dinosaurs were only about the size of a sheep."

"Okay, but how did Noah find space in the Ark for all of them?"

"Do you remember that long freight train with shipping containers that we saw one time downtown?"

"Sure."

"Do you remember how many containers were in that train?"

"No, how many."

"Well, I always like to count them," Jason answered. "There were over a hundred. And the Ark could store the contents of more than 400 such containers."

"Wow," Collin thought. "Like a huge zoo."

"Supper's ready," Carol said. "Collin, you'll need to push your book aside and go wash up."

When he came back, they all sat down at the table, and Jason led them in a short song.

"Do you think we can go to the Good Friday service tomorrow evening?" Carol wondered.

"I'm pretty sure the trial will end fairly early tomorrow afternoon," Jason remarked, "so I should be able to come home in enough time that we can all go together."

FRIDAY MORNING

THE COURTHOUSE CAFETERIA

"Well, Jason, what's new in the reporter universe this morning?" Brian knew Jason well enough by now that he'd get a pretty accurate recap.

"Well, Manning has two articles today. In the first one he starts out, 'Creationist nonsense about Noah's Flood has a short half-life after being refuted by geologists.' The other reads, 'Creationist's radioactive theory rapidly decays and leaks—only hot gas comes out.'"

"Hmm. He's pretty clever, but predictable, isn't he. What about Thomason?" Brian found these reports to be amusing.

"Here's this one by Thomason: 'Creationists and geologists try dating—and find that they are incompatible.' He's pretty clever, too. You know, his tone seems to have mellowed a bit. He seems curious about our stuff, too. I wonder if we are getting through to him. But it's annoying how he contrasts 'creationists' with 'geologists,' as if creation scientists couldn't really be geologists. Our geologists have actually done better research than mainstream geologists."

"In any case, Jason, this morning is the last chance for him to hear our evidence in the trial. I'm pretty confident our testimonies from the work of Dr. Humphreys will close with a big bang."

"Yukka, yukka, you're also pretty clever, aren't you?" Jason smirked. "Well, I'm looking beyond the debates about the Big Bang to Humphreys' theory about the Earth's magnetic field. I bet I can predict Manning's next article on that: 'Creationist is all wet about the Earth's magnetic field.'"

"Yes, it certainly is radical to think that all the matter in the Earth started off as water. Enough fun for now! Time to get serious and get to the courtroom. Your job is on the line, you know."

FRIDAY MORNING

THE COURTROOM

COSMOLOGY

Origin of the Universe

JUDGE JACOBSEN "The court is now in session."

ATTY PORTER "Your honor, the next subject concerns the Big Bang. You will recall that in the context of Darwinian evolution my witness was called first, since he could represent the work of Darwin. Mr. Cardona has similarly agreed to allow me to call my witness first to present the Big Bang theory. If you consent, we will proceed in that manner."

JUDGE JACOBSEN "Yes, go ahead."

ATTY PORTER "Then I will call now Witness 14, representing the work of Stephen Hawking, a champion of the Big Bang theory. Witness 14, please remind us about the background of this well-known cosmologist."

WITNESS 14 "Dr. Hawking received a Ph.D. from Cambridge University in applied mathematics and theoretical physics. He founded and directed the Centre for Theoretical Cosmology at the University of Cambridge. In spite of contracting Lou Gehrig's disease that eventually paralyzed him, he continued as Professor of Mathematics for 30 years. He authored *A Brief History of Time*, which sold over 25 million copies."

ATTY PORTER "What is the current scientific understanding of the origin of the universe?"

WITNESS 14 "It is the Big Bang model. It is accepted by the vast majority of scientists today."

ATTY PORTER "How did the Big Bang model come about?"

WITNESS 14 "It began with Einstein's gravitational equations of general relativity published in 1915."

ATTY PORTER "What is general relativity?"

WITNESS 14 "General relativity accounts for how gravity can affect time and space, and it provides a mathematical framework for explaining how the universe develops with time."

ATTY PORTER "Has Einstein's theory made successful predictions?"

WITNESS 14 "Yes."

ATTY PORTER "What were some of those predictions that were verified?"

WITNESS 14 "For example, the orbit of Mercury precesses around the sun, the light from distance stars is bent when passing near the sun, and clocks tick faster at higher elevations on the Earth."

ATTY PORTER "Did Einstein himself have any doubts about his equations?"

WITNESS 14 "Yes. His equations seemed to indicate that the universe had a tendency to expand, but he thought that the universe must be static."

ATTY PORTER "How did he react to this conclusion?"

WITNESS 14 "Einstein modified his equations to include a so-called cosmological constant that counteracted the tendency of the universe to expand."

ATTY PORTER "What were some reactions of other scientists?"

WITNESS 14 "Most agreed with Einstein, except for a physicist and mathematician named Alexander Friedmann."

ATTY PORTER "What did Friedmann propose?"

WITNESS 14 "Friedmann assumed that Einstein's original equations were valid without the added cosmological constant. He found corresponding solutions of those equations and predicted in 1922 that the universe must really be expanding."[129]

ATTY PORTER "Was Friedmann's prediction verified?"

WITNESS 14 "Yes. Edwin Hubble in 1929 published measurements of light from distant galaxies that demonstrated the universe is expanding."

ATTY PORTER "How did Hubble's measurements show that?"

WITNESS 14 "Hubble measured the absorption spectra of light radiated from stars and noted that their redshifts were proportional to their distance from us."

ATTY PORTER "What are absorption spectra?"

WITNESS 14 "Absorption spectra indicate how the intensity of the radiation varies with wavelength. From that information and the theory of so-called black body radiation, Hubble could estimate the star's temperature. The spectra also show wavelengths where no light is radiated. Those wavelengths, or colors, are characteristic of the chemicals in the stars and are called absorption bands."

ATTY PORTER "How did Hubble then know the distance of the stars?"

WITNESS 14 "From measurements on relatively close stars whose distance is known, he observed that the temperature and chemistry of a star determine its inherent brightness. So by measuring the apparent brightness of distant stars, he could determine their distance from us."

ATTY PORTER "And what are redshifts?"

WITNESS 14 "Hubble observed that the colors of absorption bands in each star's spectra were shifted to longer wavelengths. That is called the redshift, because red is the color with the longest visible wavelength."

ATTY PORTER "What do the redshifts indicate?"

WITNESS 14 "The redshift indicates how fast a star is going away from us. Since the observed redshifts from stars increase with their distance, we conclude that our universe is expanding in all directions."[130]

ATTY PORTER "What further conclusions were made from this observation?"

WITNESS 14 "Since the universe is expanding now, we can conclude that it was much smaller previously. Occupying a smaller volume it would also have a greater density. Einstein's equations of relativity indicated that the universe could actually have begun at a single point with enormous mass density."

ATTY PORTER "That origin is popularly called the 'Big Bang,' correct?"

WITNESS 14 "Correct."

ATTY PORTER "Did the Big Bang model lead to further predictions?"

WITNESS 14 "Yes. Since the universe would be very hot right at the Big Bang, a physicist named George Gamow concluded that there would still be radiation corresponding to a cooler temperature after the universe has expanded. He predicted that such radiation could be seen in any direction and would be more or less uniform."

ATTY PORTER "Is that called the cosmic background radiation?"

WITNESS 14 "Yes."

ATTY PORTER "When did Gamow make his prediction?"

WITNESS 14 "With some coworkers he published his prediction in 1948 and 1953. He predicted that the temperature corresponding to the background radiation would be a few degrees above absolute zero."[131]

ATTY PORTER "What is the temperature of absolute zero?"

WITNESS 14 "That is the temperature at which all physical processes stop. It is also called zero degrees kelvin and is equivalent to about minus 273 degrees centigrade or minus 460 degrees Fahrenheit."

ATTY PORTER "How was the prediction verified?"

WITNESS 14 "In 1965 Arno Penzias and Robert Wilson at Bell Laboratories were working with a large microwave antenna and noticed some microwave noise that was coming from all directions. They determined that this noise was not part of their instrumentation and concluded it must have a cosmic origin. They realized that it corresponded approximately to Gamow's prediction."

ATTY PORTER "Was further work done to quantify this radiation?"

WITNESS 14 "Yes."

ATTY PORTER "Why was that?"

WITNESS 14 "Penzias and Wilson's instruments could only measure the radiation over a relatively small range of microwave wavelengths. To determine a temperature corresponding to a very cold source, one must measure the radiation intensity over a wide range of microwave wavelengths and then compare that to the wavelength dependence of radiation expected from a so-called black body."

ATTY PORTER "Was there another reason to make more measurements of this radiation?"

WITNESS 14 "Yes. The Big Bang model predicted that there should be some small 'lumpiness' or nonuniformity in the intensity of the background radiation. This lumpiness would be left over from the nonuniform density of matter right after the Big Bang."

ATTY PORTER "How were these further measurements made?"

WITNESS 14 "NASA deployed a satellite called the Cosmic Background Explorer, or COBE for short. Measurements from a satellite eliminate most interfering sources of noise on the Earth. The satellite instruments were capable of measuring radiation with wavelengths from 3 millimeters to 300 millimeters, corresponding to microwave frequencies from 100 gigahertz down to 1 gigahertz."

ATTY PORTER "For comparison, what is the frequency of a microwave oven?"

WITNESS 14 "Microwave ovens in our homes work at 2.45 gigahertz."

ATTY PORTER "How did the COBE measurements confirm the Big Bang predictions?"

WITNESS 14 "As expected, they showed that there is some small variation in the intensity of the radiation with position in the sky. They also confirmed that the variation of the intensity of the radiation with wavelength indeed corresponds to that of an ideal black body with temperature about 2.7 degrees Kelvin."[132]

ATTY PORTER "Please remind us of what the freezing point of water is, for comparison."

WITNESS 14 "Water freezes at 273 degrees kelvin, or zero degrees centigrade."

ATTY PORTER "What is your conclusion then from all these results?"

WITNESS 14 "Successful verification of the predictions of an expanding universe, the cosmic background radiation and its characteristics all demonstrate that the Big Bang model is a reliable description of the universe and its origin."

ATTY PORTER "No further questions. Your witness, Mr. Cardona."

ATTY CARDONA "Witness 14, it is true, is it not, that the Big Bang theory originating with Friedmann assumes the universe is unbounded and has no center?"

WITNESS 14 "Yes."

ATTY CARDONA "How can the universe not have a center?"

WITNESS 14 "The universe is analogous to the surface of an expanding balloon. There is no special place on that surface; an observer at any place would notice the same characteristics."

ATTY CARDONA "Is that assumption called the cosmological principle?"

WITNESS 14 "Yes. Cosmologists such as Stephen Hawking later called it the Copernican principle."

ATTY CARDONA "Is there any scientific evidence for or against the Copernican principle that the universe is unbounded and has no center?"

WITNESS 14 "No. Both Edwin Hubble and cosmologist George Ellis admitted that the idea of a bounded universe with a center could not be disproven based on observations."[133]

ATTY CARDONA "Is it not true that Hubble also wrote that the idea of a bounded universe with a center was 'unwelcome,' and Hawking admitted that the Copernican principle of an unbounded universe without a center was 'an admixture of ideology'?"[134]

WITNESS 14 "Yes, I have read that."

ATTY CARDONA "Would Hawking's ideology be related to his religious views?"

WITNESS 14 "I suppose so."

ATTY CARDONA "I submit to you that Hawking wrote, 'I use the word "God" in an impersonal sense, like Einstein did.'[135] And Einstein often referred to himself as a disciple of the 17th century pantheist philosopher Spinoza. Hawking also wrote, 'it's my view that the simplest explanation is that there is no God. No one created the universe, and no one directs our fate.[136] Is it fair to say then that Hawking's ideology was pantheistic?"

WITNESS 14 "I suppose so."

ATTY CARDONA "It is true, is it not, that something called 'inflation' was added to the original Big Bang theory?"

WITNESS 14 "Yes."

ATTY CARDONA "Why was that?"

WITNESS 14 "'Inflation' was added to show that many possible initial conditions of the Big Bang could evolve to something like the present universe."

ATTY CARDONA "That was to avoid the need to assume that those initial conditions demonstrated some sort of fine tuning, was it not?"

WITNESS 14 "Yes."

ATTY CARDONA "Would fine tuning imply the existence of an intelligent Creator?"

WITNESS 14 "Some people would think that."

ATTY CARDONA "Please explain for us what is 'inflation.'"

WITNESS 14 "Inflation describes a temporary rapid increase in the expansion rate of the universe right after the original Big Bang."

ATTY CARDONA "Was 'inflation' also used to solve other problems?"

WITNESS 14 "Inflation solved the so-called horizon problem and the flatness problem related to the rate of expansion of the universe. It also could explain why there is so much matter in the universe."

ATTY CARDONA "What is the 'flatness problem?'"

WITNESS 14 "According to Einstein's equations, the universe would either fly apart or collapse if its expansion rate were not close to a critical rate."

ATTY CARDONA "What is the 'horizon problem?'"

WITNESS 14 "If the expansion of the universe continued at a constant rate, radiation emitted from the original Big Bang would not have had time enough to reach all parts of the universe by now and show up uniformly in all directions."

ATTY CARDONA "How much inflation is supposed to have occurred and how fast?"

WITNESS 14 "The inflation occurred in a fraction of second after the Big Bang and expanded the diameter of the universe by a factor of 10^{30}, that is a million, trillion, trillion, times."[137]

ATTY CARDONA "Is there any experimental evidence for when this inflation started and stopped or that extreme rate of expansion?"

WITNESS 14 "Those things can be calculated from the known density of matter in the universe, for example, since by itself matter tends to shrink the universe due to gravity."

ATTY CARDONA "Does that mean that something like Einstein's cosmological constant was reintroduced into his equations?"

WITNESS 14 "Yes, for the temporary increased expansion."

ATTY CARDONA "Is it not true that Einstein later regretted his use of a cosmological constant as a kind of 'fudge factor?'"

WITNESS 14 "Yes, but that was for a different reason."

ATTY CARDONA "You indicated, did you not, that measurements of the cosmic background radiation showed variations in its intensity."

WITNESS 14 "Yes, that is true."

ATTY CARDONA "What was approximately the relative magnitude of those variations?"

WITNESS 14 "Roughly one part in 100,000."

ATTY CARDONA "It is true, is it not, that most Big-Bang cosmologists expected much greater variations from the original inflation model?"[138]

WITNESS 14 "That is true. But a later inflation model could explain the data."[139]

ATTY CARDONA "Was something called 'dark matter' also introduced into the Big Bang model?"

WITNESS 14 "Yes."

ATTY CARDONA "Why was that?"

WITNESS 14 "The density of observable matter in the universe is now too small by itself to prevent runaway expansion of the universe. Also, extra matter is required to explain the observed clustering of galaxies."[140]

ATTY CARDONA "How much unobservable dark matter is required?"

WITNESS 14 "It is estimated presently that up to 90 percent of the matter in the universe is dark matter."[141]

ATTY CARDONA "And was 'dark energy' added to the original Big Bang model?"

WITNESS 14 "Yes."

ATTY CARDONA "Why was that?"

WITNESS 14 "In 1998, two independent research teams discovered from observations on NASA's Hubble Space Telescope that the rate of expansion of the universe is accelerating. Friedmann's original model only allowed for constant rates of expansion or collapse."[142]

ATTY CARDONA "What is 'dark energy?'"

WITNESS 14 "At present it is an unknown form of energy."

ATTY CARDONA "Are you aware of measurements taken of radiation from very distant stars by NASA's new James Webb Space Telescope?"

WITNESS 14 "Yes."

ATTY CARDONA "It is true, is it not, that those measurements indicate that the very distant stars have the same composition of heavy atoms as stars close to us?"

WITNESS 14 "That seems to be the case."

ATTY CARDONA "Is it not also true that those distant stars are considered to be the youngest in the universe?"

WITNESS 14 "Yes."

ATTY CARDONA "Is it correct to say that the youngest stars were not expected to have any heavy atoms since the Big Bang supposedly only produced light atoms originally?"

WITNESS 14 "That is true."

ATTY CARDONA "How then can the Big Bang model explain these measurements?"

WITNESS 14 "Scientists are working on that."

ATTY CARDONA "No further questions for Witness 14."

ATTY CARDONA "I would now like to call again Witness 11 to present the theory of Dr. Russell Humphreys on the origins of the universe. Witness 11 has already summarized Dr. Humphreys' background. Witness 11, does Dr. Humphreys' theory have anything in common with the Big Bang theory?"

WITNESS 11 "Yes. Like the Big Bang theory, his theory uses Einstein's equations of general relativity."

ATTY CARDONA "How does his theory differ from the Big Bang?"

WITNESS 11 "The Big Bang theory assumes that the universe in unbounded with no center. That is the so-called Copernican Principle. In contrast, Humphreys' theory assumes that the universe is bounded and has a center."

ATTY CARDONA "We heard Witness 14 testify that there is no observational evidence for the Copernican Principle. Is there, on the contrary, any observational evidence that the universe has a center?"

WITNESS 11 "Yes. Observations of the redshifts of stars have shown that those redshifts are clumped around multiples of certain values. The effect is somewhat smeared in the raw data but becomes dramatically apparent when the data are compensated for Earth's motion relative to the center of the cosmic background radiation. This clumping of redshifts is loosely called 'quantized redshifts.'"[143]

ATTY CARDONA "How is the center of the cosmic background radiation determined?"

WITNESS 11 "From frequency shifts of the observed microwave radiation as a function of direction."

ATTY CARDONA "What would we observe if the Earth were much further from the center of the cosmic background radiation?"

WITNESS 11 "The apparent clumping of the redshifts would totally be smeared out."

ATTY CARDONA "What is the conclusion of these data then for the model of the universe?"

WITNESS 11 "The quantized redshift data imply that the galaxies in the universe are clumped near spherical shells spaced at multiples of 1.6 and 3.1 million light years from the center of the cosmic background radiation, and the Earth is close to that center."[144]

ATTY CARDONA "Have these data been thoroughly examined?"

WITNESS 11 "Yes, the data showing quantized redshifts survived decades of peer review. They have been extended out to distances of billions of light years."

ATTY CARDONA "Was Humphreys' model able to explain how distant starlight could be seen on Earth even if the Earth is young?"

WITNESS 11 "Yes, it was."

ATTY CARDONA "How did that work out?"

WITNESS 11 "Firstly, the Bible suggested to him that there is a very great mass of water above the heavens. In particular, Psalm 148 verse 4 states: 'Praise Him you heaven of heavens, and you waters above the heavens.' Those would be the same as the 'waters above the firmament' of Genesis 1:7, where the firmament is what we call space or heaven. Humphreys supposed that those waters are now in the form of a spherical shell of ice like a huge and massive egg shell."

ATTY CARDONA "Is there any evidence for such a shell of ice?"

WITNESS 11 "Yes, his model explained the strange acceleration of Pioneer 10 and 11 spacecraft that was noticed by signals sent to them and then retransmitted back to Earth when they were already far beyond the orbit of Pluto. This acceleration was of much interest, since it is approximately equal to the so-called Hubble constant times the speed of light. No other convincing explanation has been published."[145]

ATTY CARDONA "Could Humphreys' model calculate the total mass in the spherical shell of ice from those signals from the Pioneer spacecraft?"

WITNESS 11 "Yes. From those signals he calculated that the total mass of the spherical shell is about twenty times the total mass of all the stars out to the distances seen by the Hubble Space Telescope."

ATTY CARDONA "Why is that important?"

WITNESS 11 "It allowed Humphreys to find relatively simple solutions of Einstein's equations of relativity. Those solutions indicated that time could actually stop due to the effects of gravity. We already know from experiments that clocks run slower where gravity is stronger."

ATTY CARDONA "What else did Humphreys use in his theory of distant starlight?"

WITNESS 11 "He noticed several verses from the Bible suggesting that all of the visible universe, including space, is like a fabric that has been stretched. This fabric is similar to something once called the 'ether' and now what physicists typically call the 'quantum vacuum.'"

ATTY CARDONA "What are some of those verses from the Bible?"

WITNESS 11 "For example, Isaiah 40:22, '…Who stretches out the heavens like a tent curtain, and spreads them out like a tent to dwell in.' And Psalm 104:2, 'Who stretch out the heavens like a tent curtain.'"

ATTY CARDONA "So you have testified that Humphreys' theory assumes the universe is bounded and has a center, that the Earth is near that center, that there is a massive shell of ice surrounding space, and that the fabric of space has been stretched. What was the result?"

WITNESS 11 "With his new solution to Einstein's equations, Humphreys then showed how time on Earth could stop during day four of Genesis chapter one while light from very distant stars was approaching."[146, 147]

ATTY CARDONA "Did Humphreys make a further conclusion about what he called 'the fabric of space' and what physicists call the 'quantum vacuum?'"

WITNESS 11 "Yes. Quantum field theory requires that it have a huge mass. We move through it without noticing it, somewhat like the way electrons can move freely through metals. Physicists thought the large mass of the quantum vacuum would have a huge gravitational effect, but it does not. Humphreys' model solved that problem by assuming the shell of ice above the heavens is accelerating with this fabric of space."[148]

ATTY CARDONA "Can Humphreys' model explain the cosmic background radiation?"

WITNESS 11 "Yes. He noticed a theory by physicist William Unruh published in 1976 that an accelerating object will experience blackbody radiation. Since in Humphreys' model we all are participating in the acceleration of the fabric of space, we all will notice blackbody radiation like the cosmic background radiation."[149]

ATTY CARDONA "Would you say that Dr. Humphreys proved his theory of cosmic origins that you have summarized for us?"

WITNESS 11 "No. We may never know all the physical details of cosmic origins, since they cannot be repeated. Other theories of cosmic origins exist that are generally consistent with a straightforward reading of Genesis. Nevertheless, Humphreys' theory provided some remarkable explanations of effects that had stumped others. It is also remarkable that his theory was inspired by the Bible. But as far as I know it was not a theory that could make any predictions."

ATTY CARDONA "Did Dr. Humphreys have a related theory that was also inspired by the Bible and did make successful predictions of observations?"

WITNESS 11 "Yes, that would be his theory of planetary magnetic fields."

JUDGE JACOBSEN "Mr. Cardona, I suggest that we have a short break now before taking up that topic."

THE COURTROOM HALLWAY

Brian, Jason, and Witness 11 walked out into the long hallway and found a vacant bench to sit on. Jason thought for a while and then observed, "Some Christians are trying to use the Big Bang theory to reach non-Christians. In doing so, they shoot themselves in the foot. For example, such Christians use the Big Bang as evidence that the universe had a beginning and hence that there is a God. But non-Christians often use the Big Bang itself to discredit the account of origins in Genesis. They are generally ignorant of, or not impressed by, attempts by Christian theologians and intellectuals to fit billions of years into Genesis 1."

Witness 11 added, "You mean, like the gap theory, the day age theory, the framework hypothesis, literal days separated by millions of years, the Cosmic Temple, and so on?"

"Yes." Jason continued, "Even if someone were convinced by the Big Bang that there is a God, what kind of God would He be? He would be weak and cruel in taking hundreds of millions of years to oversee and use death, violence, disease and suffering in evolution before Adam and Eve fell into temptation.

"These problems are not just exercises for the theologian, but they put real stumbling blocks in front of people considering the Christian faith. Accommodating millions of years into Genesis was supposed to remove stumbling blocks keeping Modern Man from faith in Christ.[150] In fact, however, such accommodation itself sets up stumbling blocks to believing that there is a just and yet loving God in whom we can trust."

"Very good observation, Jason. We'd better go back now," Brian said. "I hope you're okay, Witness 11. It's great stuff today, but a bit intense."

"I'm OK," replied Witness 11, " but I'd better use the rest room first."

COSMOLOGY

Planetary Magnetic Fields

JUDGE JACOBSEN "Okay, Mr. Cardona, please continue with your witness."

ATTY CARDONA "Witness 11, please explain why the topic of the magnetic fields of the planets is important."

WITNESS 11 "Firstly, planetary magnetic fields are strong evidence that the solar system is young, just as a plain reading of Genesis indicates. Secondly, there is a theory explaining the origin of these fields that was inspired directly by two passages in the Bible."

ATTY CARDONA "Is there another important feature of this theory?"

WITNESS 11 "Yes. This is a falsifiable theory. Falsifiable theories dealing with origins are rare, and scientists generally acknowledge that falsifiable theories are the strongest and best ones."

ATTY CARDONA "What distinguishes falsifiable theories from other theories?"

WITNESS 11 "Many theories are open to interpretation depending on one's bias. Some can be adjusted to fit whatever is observed. A falsifiable theory can be proven wrong by repeatable observations in the present."

ATTY CARDONA "Please describe the basic features of the earth's magnetic field."

WITNESS 11 "The magnetic field of the earth is like that of a simple bar magnet. It allows navigation by compasses. Even migrating birds are known to navigate by sensing the magnetic field. The earth's magnetic field also shields us from damage by diverting the high-energy particles from space called cosmic radiation."

ATTY CARDONA "What are the basic data concerning the earth's magnetic field?"

WITNESS 11 "The earth's magnetic field has been carefully measured for about 200 years since the time of Carl Friedrich Gauss. In that time it has decreased by more than 10 percent. The total energy in the magnetic field is presently decreasing at a rate of 50 percent about every 1,500 years."[151]

ATTY CARDONA "What causes the earth's magnetic field?"

WITNESS 11 "Scientists agree that the field is associated with electrical currents flowing in the core of the earth."

ATTY CARDONA "What are the main characteristics of the core?"

WITNESS 11 "The diameter of the core is about half that of the entire earth. It is mostly liquid, and its electrical resistivity is similar to that of molten iron."

ATTY CARDONA "What is important about the core's resistivity?"

WITNESS 11 "Just as with electrical current passing through any resistor such as in a toaster, the resistivity causes heating. That heating reduces the amount of energy stored in the magnetic field."

ATTY CARDONA "What is the conventional model for the earth's magnetic field?"

WITNESS 11 "Most scientists assume that heat flow and motion of the liquid in the core can sustain the required currents for billions of years by means of a type of electric generator called a dynamo. The main source of energy for the liquid motion is assumed to be the rotation of the earth about its axis."

ATTY CARDONA "Has anyone made a relevant theory, computer simulation, or experimental model of such a dynamo that could sustain the earth's magnetic field for billions of years?"

WITNESS 11 "Not to my knowledge."[152]

ATTY CARDONA "How long have people been working on dynamo models?"

WITNESS 11 "At least 50 years. Scale models using liquid sodium have been investigated at the University of Maryland for more than 20 years without any result that I know of that is relevant for the Earth's magnetic field."

ATTY CARDONA "Are there any data refuting the dynamo idea?"

WITNESS 11 "Yes, for example the measured magnetic field of Mercury and magnetization of rocks on the Moon."

ATTY CARDONA "How do those refute the dynamo model?"

WITNESS 11 "A dynamo model requires both a liquid core and significant rotation. Both the Moon and Mercury rotate about their axes too slowly for a dynamo, once a month for the Moon and once every two Earth months for Mercury."

ATTY CARDONA "Are there other examples?"

WITNESS 11 "Yes. The magnetic axes of both Uranus and Neptune are not nearly aligned with their rotation axes. A dynamo would require alignment of those axes."

ATTY CARDONA "What is the theory that was inspired by the Bible?"

WITNESS 11 "That theory hypothesizes that all the material in the solar system was originally water."

ATTY CARDONA "What part of the Bible leads to that conclusion?"

WITNESS 11 "Physicist Russell Humphreys noticed 'the Spirit of God was hovering over the face of the waters' in Genesis 1 verse

2; 'let the dry land appear' in Genesis 1 verse 9; and 'by the word of God the heavens were of old, and the earth standing out of water and in the water,' in Second Peter 3 verse 5."

Atty Cardona "What connection does water have with magnetic fields?"

Witness 11 "If the spins of the two hydrogen nuclei in each water molecule were lined up at the time of creation, then the water would have a large magnetic field."

Atty Cardona "What would happen then?"

Witness 11 "After creation, the spins would randomize by thermal collisions, but by the laws of physics that randomization would cause electrical currents to flow. In the absence of significant electrical resistance, the quantity called magnetic flux would be conserved. Even when water was changed to some other material, such as the dry land of Genesis 1 verse 9, the flux would be conserved. The total magnetic flux of any object would then initially be the same as the flux of the same mass of water from which it was made."

Atty Cardona "What is the consequence of that theory for the total magnetic flux of each of the planets?"

Witness 11 "The total magnetic flux of any planetary body decays due to resistive losses in its core. Nevertheless, its flux could never be higher than its flux calculated from its equivalent mass of water with the spins of the hydrogen nuclei all aligned. In this theory, that flux is called the body's created flux."[153]

Atty Cardona "Were comparisons then made between this theory and data from spacecraft flybys and other measurements?"

Witness 11 "Yes, they are shown in this diagram."

Atty Cardona "I will enter it into the record. What does this diagram show?"

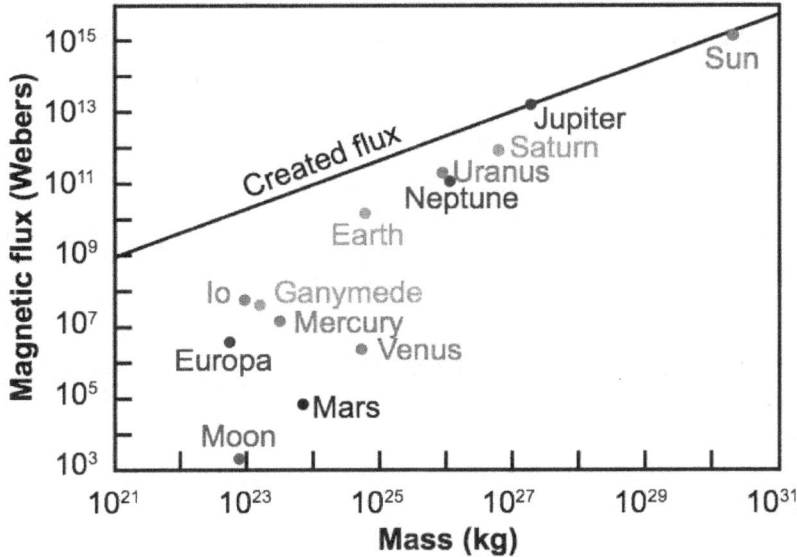

Exhibit 8. *Measured data and theoretical created flux
for solar system bodies*[154]

WITNESS 11 "All of the data are at or below the value of the original created flux determined from the theory. If any of the measured data had exceeded the theoretical created flux for a body that would have falsified the water-origin theory."

ATTY CARDONA "Were any 'fudge factors' used in the theory to avoid falsification?"

WITNESS 11 "No, none."

ATTY CARDONA "Why are the magnetic fluxes for smaller bodies much lower than their created fluxes?"

WITNESS 11 "According to the theory, the decay rate of the flux is proportional to the resistivity of the body's core divided by the square of the core's diameter. Smaller bodies have smaller cores in general, so their decay rates are faster."

ATTY CARDONA "Is the present decay rate of the earth's magnetic field consistent with Humphreys' theory and what is known about the diameter of the earth's core and its resistivity?"

WITNESS 11 "Yes."

ATTY CARDONA "What is your conclusion from the data?"

WITNESS 11 "The data do not falsify Humphreys' water-origin theory but rather strongly validate it."

ATTY CARDONA "Is there any evidence that the direction of the Earth's magnetic field has reversed in the past?"

WITNESS 11 "Yes."

ATTY CARDONA "How are reversals in the direction of the field observed?"

WITNESS 11 "When rocks are formed, the direction of the local magnetic field present during the cooling of the rocks is preserved in the magnetization of the rocks."

ATTY CARDONA "Where are these reversals observed?"

WITNESS 11 "Cores taken from drilling through rock layers exhibit alternating direction of the rock magnetization as one goes deeper from the surface. Reversals are also common near ridges that run along ocean floors near the middle of oceans. The direction of magnetization makes a well-known pattern of stripes in the ocean floor as one moves away from the central ridge."

ATTY CARDONA "What would cause these 'stripes,' as you call them?"

WITNESS 11 "It is generally agreed that molten rocks are formed by volcanic action near the central ridges. The rock material then cooled down as it flowed in both directions away from the central ridge. The local magnetic field must have changed direction several times during this process."

ATTY CARDONA "Can the conventional dynamo model explain such reversals?"

WITNESS 11 "In principle, yes. Reversals in the direction of the magnetic field are an inherent feature of dynamos."

ATTY CARDONA "How fast can the field reverse in a dynamo model?"

WITNESS 11 "It is expected that several thousands of years are required."

ATTY CARDONA "Is there any evidence for relatively rapid reversals of planetary magnetic fields?"

WITNESS 11 "Yes. The magnetic field at the surface of the sun reverses direction every 11 years."

ATTY CARDONA "What are the observed time intervals between the reversals of the Earth's magnetic field?"

WITNESS 11 "According to the conventional identification of the ages of the rocks, the time intervals between reversals were very erratic, ranging from about 200,000 years to about 30 million years."[155]

ATTY CARDONA "How many field reversals in total have been documented?"

WITNESS 11 "Roughly fifty."

ATTY CARDONA "How fast would the reversals have to have occurred to fit into the timescale of Noah's flood?"

WITNESS 11 "The flood lasted roughly a year, so an average time between reversals of about one week would be required for about 50 reversals."

ATTY CARDONA "Does the theory from Dr. Humphreys account for such rapid reversals in the Earth's magnetic field?"

WITNESS 11 "Humphreys extended his original theory to allow for large heat flows and transient electric currents near the surface of the Earth's core that might be expected during the upheavals of Noah's flood."

ATTY CARDONA "What was the main result of this extension of the theory?"

WITNESS 11 "The theory then predicted that the local magnetic field at the surface of the Earth could reverse rapidly, as fast as in one week."

ATTY CARDONA "When was such a prediction made?"

WITNESS 11 "In a paper published in 1986."[156]

ATTY CARDONA "Was any evidence later found for such rapid reversals?"

WITNESS 11 "Yes. In 1989 a paper was published demonstrating a field reversal in about two weeks or less."[157]

ATTY CARDONA "Where was this reversal observed?"

WITNESS 11 "In overlapping lava flows at Steens Mountain in southeastern Oregon."

ATTY CARDONA "How was the time interval between the various lava flows determined?"

WITNESS 11 "The volcano there had spewed out many separate lava flows that came from the same basic event."

ATTY CARDONA "Was other evidence for rapid reversals published later?"

WITNESS 11 "Yes. The main author of the 1989 paper, Robert Coe, along with other coworkers published further evidence in 1995 and 2011."[158,159]

ATTY CARDONA "What is your conclusion from these data?"

WITNESS 11 "The existing data strongly confirm the theory of Dr. Humphreys that explains how many reversals of the Earth's magnetic field could have occurred during a worldwide flood at Noah's time."

ATTY CARDONA "No further questions. Your witness, Mr. Porter."

ATTY PORTER "You mentioned, did you not, that no relevant computer simulation of a dynamo has ever been demonstrated to explain the Earth's magnetic field."

WITNESS 11 "That is correct."

ATTY PORTER "Are you not aware of a publication in 1995 of a supercomputer simulation of 40,000 years of a dynamo model that exhibited a field reversal in a few thousand years?"[160]

WITNESS 11 "Yes, I have seen that publication."

ATTY PORTER "Why would that simulation not be relevant?"

WITNESS 11 "That simulation assumed a resistance of the fluid core less than one-tenth of that known about the actual core. The simulation also assumed fluid velocities that are probably thousands of times too slow to produce rapid field reversals."[161]

ATTY PORTER "You also mentioned that the magnetic axes of Uranus and Neptune are presently misaligned with their axes of rotation, correct?"

WITNESS 11 "Correct."

ATTY PORTER "Is it not true that such misalignment during a field reversal would be expected from the dynamo model?"

WITNESS 11 "That is probably true."

ATTY PORTER "Could that mean then that both Uranus and Neptune are presently going through the process of a field reversal?"

WITNESS 11 "According to conventional theorists, field reversals are typically separated by millions of years, while the duration of a reversal in a dynamo model supposedly takes a few thousand years. So the probability of two simultaneous but unrelated reversals is extremely small. In addition, dynamo theorists explain the present rapid decay of the Earth's magnetic field also as part of an on-going field reversal. That makes three simultaneous field reversals, which is even less probable."

ATTY PORTER "Are you aware that Robert Coe, the author you mentioned, published a paper with others in 2014 in which he retracted the evidence of rapid field reversals promoted in his earlier papers?"[162]

WITNESS 11 "Yes, I am aware of that 2014 publication."

ATTY PORTER "What do you conclude from his retraction?"

WITNESS 11 "First of all, Coe reported in 2014 results that used a relatively new technique for measuring rock magnetization. His earlier results used a well-tested technique used for about 75 years in hundreds of other studies. More revealing, the paper claimed that his earlier results were 'misinterpreted by creationists in their attempts to reconcile the geological and biblical time scales.' It would seem that Coe had been under intense peer pressure not to give any validity to creation science."[163]

ATTY PORTER "No further questions."

JUDGE JACOBSEN "Counsel, do either of you have any more witnesses to call?"

ATTY CARDONA "No, your honor."

ATTY PORTER "Neither do I, your honor."

JUDGE JACOBSEN "All right, let's break now for lunch and resume at 2:00 PM. Then the court will entertain your closing arguments."

Brian got Jason and Witness 11 together and said, "Let's go out to the Watering Hole restaurant again. I've already prepared my closing arguments and the afternoon's session won't start until 2:00, so we can have a leisurely lunch. Witness 11, I really appreciate your efforts yesterday and today."

FRIDAY NOON

THE WATERING HOLE

"Jason, are you going to get a burrito again?" Brian asked.

"No, this time I'll go for the Poorboy sandwich. I'm sure it's tasty and I've got lots of bills to pay."

"Oh, come now, let's not spoil the mood. Don't you think the testimonies went well this morning?"

"Yeah," Jason remarked, "especially the testimony about the planetary magnetic fields. You could've almost left out everything else! That was so good."

"Nevertheless, we needed to counter the other side's views about biology and geology," Brian said.

"You know," Jason observed, "Christians need to understand that cosmological evolution also goes hand in hand with geological evolution and biological evolution. They really are inseparable."

Witness 11 then remarked, "It's all very religious, isn't it. When someone confronted one famous proponent of the Big Bang with the idea that other explanations existed for the cosmic background radiation besides the Big Bang, he just said, 'I think I'll stick with the good old Big Bang.' For him, the Big Bang was his good old-time religion. And, like you fellows have been saying, that religion is just pantheism."

Turning to Brian, Witness 11 continued, "This morning you pointed out quite well how the Big Bang theory needs to keep adding things like the cosmological constant, inflation, dark matter and dark energy to prop itself up. It's just like the way that they propped up Ptolemy's model of the solar system for centuries by adding more and more epicenters as needed. Band-Aids for sure."

Brian then remarked, "I consider Dr. Humphreys to be somewhat akin to a modern Galileo. Galileo had to fight ideas in the Church that came from people in the universities who were holding onto Aristotle and Ptolemy. Similarly today, Humphreys is fighting ideas rampant in the Church that come from non-Christians in the universities. I'm so grateful you could present his work here, Witness 11. When are you heading home?"

"I'm planning on leaving tomorrow morning. I want to get home for Easter."

"Then would you like to come with me this evening to a Good Friday service?" Brian said.

"Yes, I would like that," Witness 11 replied.

FRIDAY AFTERNOON

THE COURTROOM

The Attorneys' Closing Arguments

JUDGE JACOBSEN "The court is now in session. Mr. Cardona, are you ready to present your closing arguments?"

ATTY CARDONA "Yes, your honor."

JUDGE JACOBSEN "Please proceed."

ATTY CARDONA "We have shown in this trial that my client, Jason Radcliffe, has suffered viewpoint discrimination from the defendant, the Branchburg school board, by terminating him from his position as science teacher.

"The defendant admitted that my client was a capable teacher and had not deviated from his duties to present the school's science material faithfully in the classroom. They only claimed that he had introduced what they called 'inappropriate material' into his class by making certain books on creation science available in a classroom library.

"They could show no evidence of any coercion of his students to either look at those books or to believe the information presented in those books. Not only so, but we have shown that one of the books my client placed in his classroom library even presented a viewpoint in opposition to that of the creation science books. He testified that he did that to help the students learn how to think critically about what they read if they chose to do so.

"We have also gone at great lengths in this trial to demonstrate that the material in the creation science books my client placed in his classroom library was worthy of consideration. In fact, we have demonstrated how these materials provide superior explanations of data on the origin of life, the origin of new species, the origin of fossils and worldwide geologic strata, radioactive decay and measurements from planetary spacecraft. We have also demonstrated that majority theories of origins such as the Big Bang theory are full of 'fudge factors' and speculation about unobservables.

"Scientific investigation of origins is in some ways like forensic science in that past events cannot be repeated. Nevertheless, we have shown that scientific theories based on clues from the Bible have actually predicted what was later observed. Such theories involve mitochondrial DNA, radioactive decay and planetary magnetic fields.

"In summary, viewpoint discrimination is prohibited by law, and hence my client is entitled to reinstatement as science teacher at Branchburg High School. I would like to reserve the remainder of my time."

Judge Jacobsen "Mr. Porter, you may present your closing arguments."

Atty Porter "My opponent has admitted that most of the books inserted by the plaintiff in his classroom library were inspired by the Bible. My client provided evidence that one actually presented an openly religious message. A public school must be careful not to promote, or to appear to promote, any particular religion due to its obligation to separate church from state.

"In particular, we have seen in this trial how the authors of the books in question have attempted to propagate their religion. They did so by injecting the Bible into all sorts of wild pseudoscience, such as a water origin of the Earth, a worldwide Flood, multi-million-fold changes in the known decay rates of radioactive elements, and even the idea that the universe is like some gigantic piece of fabric.

"In addition, we have shown that creationist explanations have been discredited, such as the so-called 'water vapor canopy model' and the breached dam origin of the Grand Canyon. Our witnesses, on the other hand, have presented well-established explanations for natural phenomena.

"In summary, my client was perfectly justified in their action to terminate the employment of the plaintiff."

JUDGE JACOBSEN "Mr. Cardona, you may present a rebuttal with your remaining time."

ATTY CARDONA "You may recall, your honor, the testimony of our witness concerning the source of water for the Flood and for formation of the Grand Canyon. Creation scientists are continually evaluating their theories against new data as it becomes available. They often develop even stronger theories as a result. On the other hand, we have seen in this trial the resistance of mainstream scientists to consider fairly such theories.

"I have also shown in this trial that anti-theistic, even pantheistic, religion is inspiring the presuppositions behind mainstream theories of origins. Creation science is no more religious than those theories. The fact that the majority of scientists may propagate such theories does not justify mocking and excluding creation science as pseudoscience.

"I submit to you again that the defendant has similarly committed viewpoint discrimination, even religious discrimination, in terminating the employment of my client on the basis of the religion expressed in the books in my client's classroom library. A public school cannot legally favor one religion over another. The first amendment of the constitution of the United States also guarantees to my client free expression of his religion, provided that he does not force it on his students."

Judge Jacobsen "All right, if there are no further items for this court to consider, the court will be adjourned until Monday morning, at which time a decision will be made in this case."

THE COURTROOM HALLWAY

Brian walked out to the hallway with Jason, at which point Jason remarked, "You know, it would be good if the judge really bought your argument about how the speculations of mainstream scientists about origins are basically religious."

"Well, yes," Brian said, "he said so in his finding on Tuesday morning. But what of it?"

"Because," Jason reasoned, "he surely must also agree with your argument just now that a public school cannot favor one religion over another. So logically it would follow that public schools should have creation science textbooks as part of any curriculum that also uses mainstream science books dealing with origins."

"Very logical, indeed," observed Brian. "That's no doubt one reason Richard Lewontin, whom I mentioned in my opening statement, didn't want to let a Divine Foot in the door. A favorable decision for us in this case would be like that Divine Foot in the door. Our opponents would then surely fight tooth and nail to prevent anything further."

"Yeah, just like religious fanatics," Jason said. They both laughed.

"Meanwhile, like a good religious fanatic," Brian said, "I'm heading straight over to our church in Fullerton this evening with Witness 11 for the Good Friday service. Will you be able to make it to your church also?"

"Yes," Jason replied, "Easter without Good Friday is like roses without thorns."

"By the way," Jason wondered, "have you ever thought why it should be called 'Good' Friday?'"

"Yes, in fact," Brian replied. "Remember the story of the rich young ruler, how he asked Jesus, 'Good Teacher, what good thing shall I do that I may have eternal life?' And Jesus replied that 'no one is good but One, that is, God.' So on Good Friday, the only One who is good did the one good thing that we might have eternal life; namely, dying on the cross to pay for our sin."

"Very nice," Jason concluded.

SATURDAY AFTERNOON

THE RADCLIFFE FAMILY LIVING ROOM

Jason and Carol sat on the sofa reading after lunch while Collin and his friend, Brad, played outside. Jason looked up and remarked, "You know, Carol, it's become fashionable to assume that our universe is just one of many. It's comical, really. That's because of so-called 'fine tuning,' the observation that so many physical constants are just right for life.

"Since they assume our universe came about by chance, and since it's *so* improbable for *so* many things – like the mass of the sun and its distance from the Earth – to be *so* precisely tuned to what's needed for life, they then try to conclude that there must be many other unfortunate universes with other physical constants."

"What brings that up?" Carol asked.

"I started thinking about it yesterday during the testimonies about the origin of the universe."

"Well, so what?"

"I was also thinking how improbable it was that God put you and me together – like He fine-tuned everything just for us – and there's a lot of unfortunate people out there." Jason smiled and gave Carol a mischievous wink.

"You're such a hopeless romantic, my love."

"Well, it's true, isn't it."

Just then, Collin ran in from outside and shouted, "Mommy, Daddy, there's a big crowd coming down the street. They have some signs, too. One of them said 'Jason Radcliffe is a…' and I couldn't read the rest of it."

Jason went over to the window and took a look. In front of the crowd was Stuart, his former student, who complained about one of his books to the principal. He recognized two teachers from Branchburg High also. When they got up to the small lawn in front of his apartment, they started shouting, "Ho, ho, this we know, Jason Radcliffe has got to go."

One of the students threw two tennis balls at their living room window, but fortunately didn't break it. Jason turned to Carol and said, "Don't bother to look out the window. The signs are too disgusting."

Then he looked again and said, "Look at that: behind the crowd are the two reporters who covered the trial, Manning and Thomason. I wonder how they found out about this."

"What's going to happen, Daddy? Are they going to hurt us?" Collin asked.

"I don't know. Maybe not too likely, with the reporters there. I'll lock the door anyway. But for right now, we'll go in the kitchen and pray to the Lord that they don't do anything more that they will regret later. God surely sees."

EASTER SUNDAY MORNING

BRANCHBURG CHURCH OF THE OPEN DOOR

During the sermon, Jason's pastor preached from the gospel of John chapter 10 where Jesus told his followers that He is the Good Shepherd who willingly gave His life for the sheep.

"Not only did Jesus tell us that He is the Good Shepherd, not only did he lay down His life for the sheep," Pastor Dan emphasized, "but Jesus also said that He is the door for the sheep.

"Jesus is the door to salvation, just like the door to Noah's Ark. When God called Noah and his family into the Ark, they had to go into the Ark through that door as the *only* way they could be saved from the Flood."

Pastor Dan also likened the Flood to God's judgment on sin, the judgment that Jesus endured on the cross. "Jesus endured the judgment of sin on that dark crucifixion Friday. But his resurrection proves to us that He overcame sin and death and judgment. His resurrection proves that we too can experience new life – eternal life – through faith in Jesus!"

He concluded by comparing faith in Christ to Noah and his family, who trusted in God as they entered the Ark through its door and were saved from the destruction of the Flood. "When they went out of the Ark by that same door, they also partook of a new life after the Flood. They had a new beginning!"

After the last hymn and the benediction, Jason turned around and spotted Mr. Thomason standing near the rear door of the church. Jason went over to greet him, and Thomason quickly asked, "Could you introduce me to your pastor? I'll like to talk to him about becoming a Christian."

Jason was very surprised. "Of course, Mr. Thomason, but what's changed? This is such a wonderful surprise!"

Thomason seemed eager to explain – and eager to meet Pastor Dan. "You see, Jason, on Wednesday night your friends answered some of my questions I could never get answered as a kid in church. The trial answered more of my questions, so I've been thinking.

"Then yesterday's ugly crowd showing up at your house also showed me that evil motivates those who oppose you. It made me want to come to church this morning. Pastor Dan's sermon gave me hope that the evil I've done can be forgiven. In particular, can you forgive me for the evil reports I wrote about you and your attorney?"

Jason Replied, "Of course I can. God forgave me, so I am happy, overjoyed even, to forgive you! Follow me, let's go meet the pastor."

MONDAY MORNING

THE BRANCHBURG COURTROOM

JUDGE JACOBSEN "The court is now in session. The plaintiff has provided ample testimony that a plain reading of the Creation and Flood accounts in the Bible is as scientifically believable as any account of events in the past could be. Their witnesses have also demonstrated that the standard accounts of the origin of the Earth and universe have serious scientific flaws.

"The defendant has claimed that inappropriate religious views were expressed implicitly in most of the science books placed in the plaintiff's classroom library. The plaintiff has shown that the standard origin accounts implicitly express a different religious view. This court stands by the First Amendment to the Constitution that a school may not favor one religion over another.

"The defendant has also claimed that one of the books that the plaintiff placed in his classroom library explicitly expressed a Christian doctrine that a public school should not be teaching. It has been determined in this trial that the plaintiff did not force any of his students to read that book, nor did he promote his religious beliefs in his classroom. The court finds again, in accordance with the First Amendment, that a teacher is free to express his religion, provided that no student is intimidated by such expression or judged by his lack of agreement with any such expression by the teacher.

"Therefore, this court finds that the defendant has wrongfully terminated the employment of the plaintiff, and that the plaintiff is entitled to have his job as science teacher in Branchburg High School restored. It is so ordered. The court is now adjourned."

Reporter Henry Manning immediately approached the school board representative, and they walked out of the courtroom together. Reporter Douglas Thomason walked over to Jason and Brian and shook their hands in congratulation. "God bless you guys! I'm glad you won, and I'll keep in touch."

"Thank you, Mr. Thomason," Jason replied with a smile and a nod.

"And you can call me Brother Thomason now!" The reporter asserted.

Brian turned to Jason and suggested, "How about we go unwind a bit in the cafeteria?"

"That's a great idea but let me first send Carol a text, as well as our faithful supporter and your friend, Brandon Taylor."

MONDAY MORNING

THE COURTHOUSE CAFETERIA

After grabbing some donuts and coffee and finding a nice booth by the window, Jason observed, "This is like the parting of the Red Sea to me. This whole thing has weighed heavy on me for a long time, and now I'm free!"

"And I'm happy to have been part of it," Brian added.

"Speaking of the Red Sea," Brian ventured, "some skeptics are spreading the idea around that there's no archaeological evidence for the Exodus. Some in my church are wondering how to answer them."

"Well, do you know how to counter the skeptics' argument?" Jason asked.

"No. Do you?"

"Yes, in fact," Jason replied. "I've had a bunch of free time the past few months to read about such things. The basic problem is that people are looking at the wrong time period in Egyptian history – namely the 18th dynasty. For sure, there is no evidence of the Exodus then. But Egyptian time periods have been ballooned by nonexistent and overlapping dynasties. If you look at the history of the 12th and 13th dynasties instead, there is abundant evidence for the Exodus."[164]

"How'd you ever get interested in that?" Brian queried.

"It's related to what we have been talking about in the trial," Jason replied. "Most of academia believes that everything before the Egyptians is 'pre-history,' and not subject to historical inquiry. Instead, it's relegated to cosmological, geological and biological evolution, the domain of science.

"In fact, however, a common name for Egypt – even today in the Middle East – is Mizr or Mizraim, and Mizraim was a grandson of Noah according to Genesis chapter 10. So the events before the Egyptians are not 'pre-history,' but actually the history recorded in the early chapters of Genesis. Creation science just confirms that history."

"So, now that we've also *made history* with this trial, I think I'll go out for a round of golf," Brian concluded. "How about you?"

"I've got to pick up my son Collin and his friend, Brad, from pre-school. I'm making up for the end of last week when Brad's mom drove them to and from school for me. Maybe I'll see if they want to go to the Dale County Zoo. We can see the lions and talk about Daniel in the Lion's den."

"When will you get to celebrate with your wife?" Brian asked.

"This weekend will be a good time for that!" replied Jason.

TUESDAY MORNING

THE RADCLIFFE FAMILY KITCHEN

Jason was preparing an omelet when Carol came into the kitchen.

"I'm so sorry, love, I don't have much time to eat now," Carol said. "Our school principal called a pre-school meeting for teachers today."

"Hmm, I suppose I could guess what that might be about," Jason said. "The news from Henry Manning this morning is that the Branchburg school district is going to appeal yesterday's decision in my case."

"Oh, no! Not after all that work and the legal bills we've incurred."

"Well, I'll be calling Brian this morning to see if we can talk it over this afternoon," Jason continued.

"Please don't decide anything without me," Carol pleaded. "I've gotta go shopping on the way home, so I'll be a little later than usual."

"Don't worry, hon. Tonight we can talk over what he says."

TUESDAY AFTERNOON

THE OFFICE OF ATTORNEY BRIAN CARDONA

"I'm really sorry about this appeal," Brian kicked off the conversation. "I didn't think the school district would care so much about this case. But remember our conversation after court on Friday afternoon? This trial has attracted lots of media attention and it seems that our opposition has concluded that the judge just let a Divine Foot in the door."

"What do you suggest?" Jason asked. "I'm not sure I can even pay for all the current legal costs for quite a while."

"Don't worry about any urgency in paying me," Brian replied. "I have another idea about this appeal – aside from the money involved – if you want to consider it."

"I'm all ears. Shoot!" Jason noted a sense of optimism in Brian's voice.

"Well, for the good of our wider community, it might be better for us not to contest the appeal. That way, the appeal will be moot and the judge's decision yesterday won't be contested. It then *could* serve as valuable precedent for other Christians in similar situations.

"If we proceed to fight the appeal, we'll have to go before a three-judge panel. I think we should be very thankful for the judge we had; there aren't too many who think like him. It's certainly not obvious that we would win an appeal. Plus – to their advantage – the school district pretty much has unlimited taxpayer funds available to keep pursuing it."

"But I really liked my job at the high school," Jason objected. "And I think I was having a good influence there. It's not right."

"I'm sure that's true, Jason. But your former student, Stuart, has been stirring up trouble."

"Yeah, a couple of teachers even joined him and the others at the scene outside our home last Saturday."

"Well, go home and pray about it with Carol. I'll be praying also."

"Thanks, Brian. I can't tell you enough how much I appreciate all your incredible skill and even spiritual support. God is surely going to bless and reward you for all you do. I'll go home and talk this over with Carol."

TUESDAY EVENING

THE RADCLIFFE FAMILY APARTMENT

When Carol came home, she found Jason reading on the sofa in the living room while Collin was in his usual spot on the floor looking at his latest dinosaur book.

"So, how did your principal's pre-school meeting go?" Jason asked Carol.

"Well, your guess about the meeting was about right. The principal told the teachers that they would appeal the court ruling yesterday, 'so don't get any ideas about putting religious books in your classroom libraries,' she told us sternly." Carol mimicked the principal's stern tone and cracked a smile.

"Yeah, right," Jason commented, "meanwhile, like you told me before, you've got elementary teachers at your school who are putting books in their classroom libraries that normalize sexual experimentation."

"Yes, one of our second-grade teachers even did that. Lord, help us!" Carol exclaimed. "But that's a battle for another day. What did attorney Brian say today?"

Jason summarized his discussion with Brian before switching gears. "But I've also got some unexpected news!"

"Tell me. I could use unexpected news – especially if it's good news!"

"First of all, the Believers Legal Fund got wind of our situation and called me today. They offered to take on the appeal with their own attorneys at no cost to us."

"Wow, that is good news! But we'd still have to pay Brian for everything up 'til now, right?"

"True. That's not all, however. The Dale County Christian School called and offered me a job as a science teacher. When I told them that you are also a teacher, they offered you a job, too."

"That's certainly nice of them, isn't it? You've made us famous, haven't you, love! But that's a big decision right now. It means we'd have to move, since they're in Craigsville and that's a bit too far to commute."

"I thanked them and told them we'd think about it and get back to them if we wanted a formal offer. I suppose the salaries would be considerably lower than in the public schools here."

Carol thought for a minute and then observed, "My gracious, things are happening fast, aren't they? It would be a shame to leave all our friends here, our church and all the students we've invested our lives in. How'll we know what to do?"

"Proverbs 3 says that if we acknowledge God in all our ways, He will direct our paths. He has before, hasn't He? We should remember to pray also for our new brother Thomason. We don't know how his newspaper colleagues will respond to his new-found faith. Before I forget, though, there's one more piece of news. Do you remember my student, Peter Benson, the inquisitive one who borrowed two of my books from the classroom library? His parents called and said Peter really likes me and they hope I'll get my job back."

Collin looked up from his book and asked, "What are you talking about? Are we going to be okay? My friend Brad asked me today if we're going to be okay."

Jason replied, "Collin, we've got a lot to think about, but yes, we are going to be okay. God's got us, he takes care of us, my little buddy. Right now, though, I'm going to help Mommy unload the groceries from her car while she makes supper. After supper we'll all pray together about what God wants us to do next."

Collin jumped up from the floor. "Amen, Daddy! God's got us! Can I help you with the groceries?"

"You bet, little buddy, God's got us! Now, let's help Mommy, shall we?"

ABOUT THE AUTHOR

 Dr. John Doane is known for his work in creation science. He holds a Ph.D. in Electrical Engineering and has contributed to both scientific and religious discussions.

Dr. Doane is the author of *Let God Be True: A Christian's Guide to Origins Science,* which explores the intersection of faith and science. He has also published several technical papers on millimeter-wave technology related to fusion energy research.

After graduating from Yale University, John Doane was a Hertz Fellow at MIT where he obtained a PhD in Electrical Engineering. He has worked in millimeter-wave technology at Bell Laboratories, the Princeton Plasma Physics Laboratory and General Atomics. For many years he was on the Board of Directors for Jesus to the Communist World (which later became Voice of the Martyrs). He is a principal in DeposiTech, Inc., established by his wife to make plasma-based equipment for electronics manufacturing.

Learn more at www.religioninscience.org.

BIOGRAPHICAL POSTSCRIPT

At one of my talks on creation science, during the question-and-answer session, I noticed several audience members were as interested in my personal story as in the content of my message. To address such curiosity, I offer some biographical information below.

One day as a kid walking in the woods behind our house, I noticed lots of ferns near a little river. For some reason I thought, "Those are supposed to be millions of years old." That's about all I heard about evolution, since I never took a formal biology class. I was more interested in "dry and crisp" things like math and electricity.

In high school, I was the president of our youth fellowship at a Methodist church. I once heard a sermon there on Matthew 9, where Jesus said, "I did not come to call the righteous, but sinners, to repentance." That confused me, because I didn't think I was one of those awful people called "sinners." At the same time, I liked to say that Protestantism is good, because it teaches that everyone can know the truth from reading the Bible without the aid of doctrine from a church hierarchy. And yet I never read the Bible on my own.

As I prepared to graduate from college, I applied for a Hertz Foundation graduate student fellowship, endowed by the founder of Hertz Rental Cars. The Foundation sent Dr. Edward Teller to interview me. While Dr. Teller was famous for his work in chemistry and on hydrogen bombs, he was kind and patient with me. I was too embarrassed to apply later for a sixth year of the fellowship, but Dr. Teller insisted.

In 1965, after drifting academically and spiritually during my first year of graduate work at MIT, I went to Park Street Church in Boston. I sought out a particular youth minister who had published an article in *National Review* on "The Protestant Deformation," wherein he documented the lack of belief in traditional Christian doctrines by many pastors in mainline denominations. Instead of finding him, I was led to a gathering of seemingly ordinary, middle-aged people praying for one another. An encounter with the holiness of God at that gathering finally convicted me that I was a sinner in need of a Savior. The next day I went to the Massachusetts Bible Society and purchased a Bible.

Soon afterward, I became involved with a ministry helping Christians in communist countries. That ministry acquainted me with the testimonies of faithful Christians who proclaimed the truth of the Bible when it was not only unpopular but also very costly to them personally.

The pastor of Park Street Church at that time was Dr. Ockenga, who was also a founder of the National Association of Evangelicals and a leader in the formation of Gordon and Fuller theological seminaries. He delighted and inspired me with his Bible expositions on Sunday mornings and his application of scripture to current affairs in his Sunday evening sermons. One Sunday evening during a question-and-answer period with the graduate student fellowship, a student asked him if he believed in evolution. As I remember, he replied that if scientists accept it then he thought we should accept it also. That seemed to imply that the ideas of scientists could be more authoritative than the Bible, but I didn't think more about it at the time.

A few years later I met a medical doctor with an interest in the modern creationist movement. He introduced me to data that the magnetic field of the earth is decaying rapidly and a simple theory that seemed to explain the data based on the current flowing in the earth's core. As an electrical engineer, I found this fascinating. I gave a talk near Princeton University summarizing this theory and the supporting data. Later I encountered criticism of that theory based on reversals of the magnetic field inferred from observations of the magnetism of rocks at the bottom of oceans.

The author of the original theory tried to explain the reversals as the result of magnetostriction, whereby stress can rotate the magnetic field in a material. However, at the time my wife was also doing her Ph.D. thesis on magnetostriction and it became clear to me that magnetostriction could only rotate the field by 90-degrees, not by 180-degrees. So I stopped speaking about the earth's magnetic field for a while. A prolific creation scientist, Dr. Russell Humphreys, later demonstrated how fluid motions in the earth's core could cause reversals of the field in as quickly as a week or so during the Flood.

During this time a professor from a large university gave a talk at Bell Laboratories where I was working. He started by assuming that the earth was billions of years of years old and then tried to work back theoretically to determine the age of the universe. He concluded with a common jibe from evolutionists, mocking Bishop Ussher's determination that the earth is only about 6,000 years old. I had no understanding of how to criticize the details of his talk, and I didn't think I could get anywhere with a direct attack on his assumption about an ancient age of the earth.

So, during the question-and-answer session I pointed out an interesting fact about radiometric dating: namely, that some rocks have plenty of a certain isotope of lead but no radioactive thorium, which through decay is known to be the only source of that isotope. So, to cast doubt on the reliability of radiometric decay dating, I asked if that then showed the earth to be infinitely old. The speaker didn't like the implication that radiometric dating could be unreliable, so he replied that "one has to carefully choose which rocks one picks to do radiometric dating."

A couple years before my eldest son was scheduled to enter high school near Princeton, I visited the head of the high school science department and asked if he wanted to trade books. I could learn what they were teaching, and he could learn something about creation science. I explained that I worked for Princeton University Plasma Physics Laboratory and would be happy to give a talk to his students if he would like a speaker on this controversial topic. About a year later, the teacher did invite me to talk to a group of gifted students.

Before I came, however, the teachers had strategically given each student a one-inch-thick dossier of references supporting evolution. My talk was titled, "Creation and Evolution: Why it takes more faith to believe in evolution now than when Darwin wrote his book." I did not mention the Bible in my talk, but when I finished the talk, students brought up the Bible in their questions. I found them to be quite respectful, and they did not try to make fun of what I had said in any way. The head of the science department acknowledged that my talk had been pretty convincing, but asked me "Do you have to be a Christian if you believe in creation?" I replied that many Jews and Muslims also believe in creation, but I don't think that's what he was getting at. Most likely, he really wanted to know, "If I believe in creation, do I have to obey God and live like a Christian?"

Since then, I worked for many years at General Atomics. Our group there designed and built components for transmission of very high frequency microwaves used at laboratories working with plasmas for fusion energy research. At present I am working with copper plasmas for an application in electronics for which my wife had the vision.

When my eldest son went to college, we had been invited to the home of his affable Christian chemistry professor. Incidentally, I recently looked up some of his writings and discovered that he had a very interesting insight about miracles. Indeed, he pointed out that everything in nature is a miracle. In particular, Jesus upholds everything even now by the word of His power (Hebrews 1:3). However, this professor had also written that the evidence for an ancient earth is overwhelming and should not be controversial. He worried that teaching otherwise would put up roadblocks to Christian faith.

Actually, as this book attempts to show, evidence for a young earth is very strong and upholds the character of God and our need for a Savior.

One of the most eye-opening materials I have encountered from creation science ministries is a DVD from Answers in Genesis by Dr. Terry Mortenson entitled, "Millions of Years: Where did the idea come from?" He had a two-fold message: Firstly, evolution is not just speculation about biological origins, it also includes geological and cosmological evolution. Secondly, speculations about evolution are all based on presuppositions that originated from non-Christians with a bias against the Bible.

Most recently, the medical doctor who introduced me to creation science through the data on the magnetic field of the earth, further introduced me to the work of Baruch Spinoza. Spinoza was a 17th century pantheist who claimed that the Bible is good for promoting piety but not for understanding truth. He denied the existence of supernatural miracles and was the first to claim specifically that science and the study of truth must be separated from theology and the Bible.[165] That doctrine implies that only scientists can know the truth about the physical origins of the universe. In combination with speculations by non-Christians about billions of years, it has wreaked havoc in the Church, causing many to doubt the reliability and authority of Genesis. For that reason, I am working to promote the understanding that I hope may come from this book.

PHOTO CREDITS

Exhibit 1. http://en.wikipedia.org/wiki/File:Miller-Urey_experiment-en.svg

Exhibit 2. John Doane

Exhibit 3. https://answersingenesis.org/geology/geologic-time-scale/geologic-column/

Exhibit 4. https://answersingenesis.org/fossils/squid-fossilized-catching-dinner/

Exhibit 5. Steven A. Austin [in John Morris and Steven A. Austin, *Footprints in the Ash*, Green Forest, AR: Master Books (2003), p. 52]

Exhibit 6. Andrew A. Snelling and John Whitmore, at https://answersingenesis.org/geology/grand-canyon/fight-53-rocks/

Exhibit 7. John Whitmore, at: https://answersingenesis.org/geology/grand-canyon/coconino-sandstone-most-powerful-argument-against-flood/

Exhibit 8. D. Russell Humphreys [in "The Creation of Cosmic Magnetic Fields," Proceedings of the Sixth International Conference on Creationism, Andrew Snelling, ed., Pittsburgh, PA: Creation Science Fellowship (2008), p. 220]

Darwin's Arch before collapse: Galápagos National Park, Ecuador. Published in CBS News, NBC News, Seattle Times, etc. via Associated Press.

Darwin's Arch after collapse: Héctor Berrera, Ecuador's Ministry of the Environment. Published in USA Today, Newsweek, Daily Mail, etc.

END NOTES

Prologue

[1] From a newsletter of Far Reaching Ministries, available at: https://frmusa.org/wp-content/uploads/View-full-December-2019-Newsletter-here.pdf

[2] The courtroom format is used for rhetorical purposes and may not be completely realistic from a legal standpoint. The author does not claim to be a legal expert.

[3] Jerry Bergman, *Silencing the Darwin Skeptics* [Vol. III in "Slaughter of the Dissidents"], Southworth, WA: Leafcutter Press (2016), p. 116.

Pre-Trial Motions

[4] Available, for example, at: https://law.justia.com/cases/federal/district-courts/FSupp2/400/707/2414073/

[5] See, for example, John Doane, "Spinoza's Ghost in the Evangelical Closet," *Creation Research Society Quarterly*, Vol. 59, No. 3 (2023), pp. 128-141.

[6] Jonathan Israel, *Radical Enlightenment: Philosophy and the Making of Modernity 1650-1750*, Oxford University Press (2001), p. 160.

[7] https://abcnews.go.com/WN/Technology/stephen-hawking-religion-science-win/story?id=10830164

[8] William Barr, speech at Notre Dame University, Oct. 11, 2019. Available at https://www.americanrhetoric.com/speeches/williambarrnotredame.htm

[9] Greg Epstein, *Good Without God: What a Billion Non-Religious People do Believe*, New York: Harper (2009), p. 49.

[10] Walter Isaacson, *Einstein: His Life and Universe*, New York: Simon and Schuster (2007), pp. 388-389.

[11] Stephen Hawking, *Brief Answers to the Big Questions*, New York: Bantam Books (2018), p. 28.

[12] Francis Bacon, *The Advancement of Learning* (1906 Oxford edition) p. 46 (Book I, part VI.16), cited in Terry Mortenson, *The Great Turning Point: The Church's Catastrophic Mistake on Geology—Before Darwin*, Green Forest AR: Master Books (2004), p. 21.

[13] Ibid, p. 229 (Book II, part XXV.16), cited in Mortenson, op. cit., p. 22.

[14] Ibid, p 43 (Book I, part VI. 9-11), cited in Mortenson, op. cit., p. 22.

[15] For example, Theodosius Dobzhansky, "Nothing in Biology Makes Sense Except in the Light of Evolution", *American Biology Teacher*, Vol. 35, No. 3 (1973), pp. 125–129.

[16] Terry Mortenson, *The Great Turning* Point, op. cit, pp. 224-227.

[17] Derek Ager, *The New Catastrophism: The Importance of the Rare Event in Geological History*, Cambridge University Press (1993), p. xi.

[18] Derek Ager, *The New Catastrophism: The Importance of the Rare Event in Geological History*, Cambridge University Press (1993), p. xi.

[19] Stephen W. Hawking and George F. R. Ellis, *The Large-Scale Structure of Space-Time*, Cambridge: The Cambridge University Press (1973), p. 134. Quoted in D. Russell Humphreys, *Starlight and Time*, Green Forest, AR: Master Books (1994).

[20] Ibid.

[21] D Russell Humphreys, "The Battle for a Cosmic Center," Institute for Creation Research, *Impact*, #350, August 2002. www.icr.org/article/battle-for-cosmic-center/

[22] Matthew 6:22-23.

[23] See, for example, Jerry Bergman, "Censorship in Publishing On the Rise," Chapter 2 in *Censoring the Darwin Skeptics*, [Vol. III in "Slaughter of the Dissidents"], Port Orchard, WA: Leafcutter Press (2018), pp. 37-72.

[24] See, for example, R. M. Cornelius and John D. Morris, *Scopes: Creation on Trial*, Green Forest, AR: Master Books (1999), pp. 36-43.

[25] https://jgmachen.org/2011/06/06/machen-and-creation-in-six-days/.

[26] William Lane Craig, *In Quest of the Historical Adam*, Grand Rapids, MI: Eerdmans (2021), p. 13.

[27] John Lennox, *Seven Days that Divide the World: The Beginning According to Genesis and Science*, Grand Rapids, MI: Zondervan (2011), p. 86.

[28] Francis Collins, in "God vs. Science," *Time Magazine*, Nov 13, 2006.

[29] Mark Noll, *The Scandal of the Evangelical Mind*, Grand Rapids, MI: Eerdmans (2022).

[30] Lisa Grunwald, "The Scopes Trial Is Still With Us," *Time*, April 12, 2024.

[31] Michael Zimmerman, "Debunking New Myths," Creation/Evolution Journal, Vol 9, No. 1 (1989), available at: https://ncse.ngo/debunking-new-myths

[32] Job 41:18-21.

The Trial Begins

[33] Richard Lewontin, "Billions and billions of demons," *The New York Review of Books*, 9 January 1997, p. 31. Italics were in the original.

[34] John Morris and Frank Sherwin, *The Fossil Record*, Dallas, TX: Institute for Creation Research (2010). D. Russell Humphreys and M. De Spain, *Earth's Mysterious Magnetism*, Chino Valley, AZ: Creation Research Society (2016). Don DeYoung, *Thousands...Not Billions*, Green Forest, AR: Master Books (2005). Timothy Clarey, *Carved in Stone: Geological Evidence for a Worldwide Flood*, Dallas, TX: Institute for Creation Research (2020). John Sanford, *Genetic Entropy*, 4th Edition, Canandaigua, NY: FMS Publications (2014). Carol Hill, Gregg Davidson, Tim Helble and Wayne Ranney, eds., *The Grand Canyon: Monument to an Ancient earth*, Grand Rapids, MI: Kregel Publications (2016).

Biology

[35] Stanley L. Miller, "Production of Amino Acids Under Possible Primitive Earth Conditions," *Science*, Vol. 117 (1953), pp. 528–9.

[36] Proverbs 18:17

[37] Dr. Lee Cronin vs Dr. James Tour Debate at Harvard Cambridge Faculty Roundtable on the Origin of Life, Nov. 15, 2023: https://www.youtube.com/watch?v=6GDv4f2zUus

[38] Suzan Mazur, *The Altenberg 16: An Exposé of the Evolution Industry*, Berkeley, CA: North Atlantic Books (2010), p. vii.

[39] R. N. Melchor, S. de Valais, and J. F. Genise, "Bird-like fossil footprints from the Late Triassic," *Nature*, 417 [6892] (2002), pp. 936-938. Cited in Morris and Sherwin, op. cit.

[40] G. Niedzwiedzki et al, "Tetrapod trackways from the early Middle Devonian period of Poland," *Nature*, 463 [7277] (2010), pp. 43-48. Cited in Morris and Sherwin, op. cit.

[41] Martin Lubenow, *Bones of Contention: A Creationist Assessment of Human Fossils*, Grand Rapids, MI: Baker Books (1992), p. 178.

[42] Ibid, p. 178.

[43] Ibid, p. 179.

[44] Ibid, p. 178.

[45] Ibid, p. 181.

[46] Morris and Sherwin, op. cit., pp. 92-94.

[47] Doug Sharp and Jerry Bergman, eds., *Persuaded by the Evidence: True Stories of Faith, Science & the Power of a Creator*, Green Forest, AR: Master Books (2008), pp. 147-153.

[48] Nathaniel Jeanson and Jeffrey Tomkins, "Genetics Confirms the Recent, Supernatural Creation of Adam and Eve, in Terry Mortenson, ed., *Searching for Adam: Genesis and the Truth About Man's Origin*, Green Forest, AR: Master Books (2016), pp. 287-330.

[49] Jerry Bergman, *"Useless Organs: The Rise and Fall of a Central Claim of Evolution,"* Tulsa, OK: Bartlett Publishing (2019).

[50] Jeanson and Tomkins, op. cit., p. 316.

[51] Nathaniel Jeanson, *Replacing Darwin: The New Origin of Species*, Green Forest, AR: Master Books (2017), pp. 192-193.

[52] Dennis Venema and Scot McKnight, *Adam and the Genome: Reading Scripture after Genetic Science*, Grand Rapids, MI: Brazos Press (2017).

[53] Ibid, p. 32.

[54] Jeanson and Tomkins, op. cit., p. 296.

[55] Ibid.

[56] https://www.reuters.com/article/scienceNews/idUS-TRE4AH1P020081118/

Geology

[57] John Morris and Frank Sherwin, *The Fossil Record*, Dallas, TX: Institute for Creation Research (2010), p. 41.

[58] Ibid, p. 53.

[59] Ibid, p. 38; Timothy Clarey, *Carved in Stone: Geological Evidence for a Worldwide Flood*, Dallas, TX: Institute for Creation Research (2020). pp. 301-33.

[60] Morris and Sherwin, op. cit., pp. 113-115; "Living Fossils Wall Chart," *Answers Magazine*, Vol. 6, No. 1 (2010).

[61] Morris and Sherwin, op. cit., p. 115, p. 72, p. 82.

[62] Kevin Anderson, *Echoes of the Jurassic*, Chino Valley, AZ: Creation Research Society (2010), cited in Clarey, op. cit., p. 455.

[63] Clarey, op. cit., pp. 455-457.

[64] Morris and Sherwin, op. cit., p. 116.

[65] Ibid, p. 117.

[66] https://answersingenesis.org/racism/its-not-just-black-and-white/

[67] D. G. Pearson et al, "Hydrous mantle transition zone indicated by ringwoodite included within diamond," *Nature*, 507 [7491] (2014), pp. 221-224, cited in Clarey, op. cit., p. 37.

[68] Clarey, op. cit., pp. 208-209.

[69] Ibid, pp. 54-55, and private communication.

[70] Ibid, pp. 250-251.

[71] Ibid, pp. 251-252.

[72] Ibid, p. 425.

[73] Ibid, p. 430.

[74] Ibid, pp. 427-428.

[75] John Morris and Steven Austin, *Footprints in the Ash: The Explosive Story of Mt. St. Helens*, Green Forest, AR: Master Books (2003), pp. 82-88.

[76] Clarey, op. cit., pp. 431-435.

[77] Morris and Austin, op. cit., pp. 52-53.

[78] Andrew Snelling, "The Fight for 53 Rocks," Dec. 29, 2021, available at: https://answersingenesis.org/geology/grand-canyon/fight-53-rocks/

[79] Ibid.

[80] Terry Mortenson, *The Great Turning Point*, op. cit., pp. 224-227

[81] Interview with Dr. Ron Neller, available at: https://creation.com/nl/podcasts/flood-expert-finds-evidence-for-noahs-flood

[82] Tas Walker, "Eroding Ages: If our continents were old, they would no longer be here," *Creation*, Vol. 22, No. 3 (2000), pp. 18-21.

[83] Clarey, op. cit., pp. 32-35.

[84] Don Batten, "The Age of Arches," *Creation* Vol. 40, No. 4 (2018), p. 23, updated Oct. 7, 2020.

[85] Darwin's Arch is very close to a small island also named after Darwin. Both are very remote, requiring a day's journey by boat.

[86] Andrew Snelling, "The Fight for 53 Rocks," op. cit.

[87] For example, Jerry Bergman, *Slaughter of the Dissidents*, Vols. I, II, III, Southworth, WA: Leafcutter Press (2008, 2016, 2018).

[88] Carol Hill et al, *Grand Canyon: Monument to an Ancient Earth*, op. cit., p. 70

[89] Ibid, p. 69.

[90] Ibid, pp. 154-157.

[91] Ibid, p. 158.

[92] Ibid, pp. 175-176.

[93] Clarey, op. cit., p. 46.

[94] John Whitmore, "Coconino Sandstone—The Most Powerful Argument Against the Flood?," *Answers*, available at: https://answersingenesis.org/geology/grand-canyon/coconino-sandstone-most-powerful-argument-against-flood/

[95] Ibid.

[96] Clarey, op. cit., pp. 342-343.

[97] John Baumgardner, "Runaway Subduction as the Driving Mechanism for the Genesis Flood," Proceedings of the Third International Conference on Creationism, R. Walsh ed., Pittsburgh, PA: Creation Science Fellowship (1994), pp. 63-75.

[98] Clarey, op. cit., pp.114-151.

[99] Carol Hill et al, op. cit, p. 112.

[100] Clarey, op. cit., pp. 136-137.

[101] Terry Mortenson, "*The Grand Canyon, Monument to an Ancient Earth*: The Deceptions Continue," *Answers Research Journal* Vol. 13 (2020), pp. 275-276.

[102] Ibid, p. 277.

[103] Don DeYoung, *Thousands…Not Billions*, Green Forest, AR: Master Books (2005), pp. 50-51.

[104] Ibid, p. 54.

[105] Ibid, p. 49.

[106] Ibid, p. 55-57.

[107] Ibid, pp. 56-58.

[108] Ibid, p. 58.

[109] See Mike Riddle, "Doesn't Carbon-14 Dating Disprove the Bible?" *The New Answers Book 1*, Green Forest, AR: Master Books (2006), pp. 77-87, and references therein.

[110] Don DeYoung, op. cit., p. 59.

[111] Ibid, pp. 66-67.

[112] Ibid, p. 71.

[113] Ibid, pp. 72-76.

[114] Ibid, p. 75.

[115] Ibid, pp. 72, 77.

[116] Ibid, pp. 77-78.

[117] For example, Isaiah 40:22, 64:1, 34:4 and Revelation 6:14.

[118] Russell Humphreys, "New mechanism for accelerated removal of excess radiogenic heat," Proceedings of the Eighth International Conference on Creationism, John Whitmore, ed., Pittsburgh, PA: Creation Science Fellowship (2018), pp. 731-739.

[119] Don DeYoung, op. cit., pp. 125-129.

[120] Ibid, pp. 132-134.

[121] Ibid, pp. 134-136.

[122] Ibid, pp. 126-127.

[123] Ibid.

[124] Ibid.

[125] Carol Hill et al, op. cit., p. 92.

[126] Ibid., pp. 93, 95.

[127] Ibid, p. 94.

[128] Andrew Snelling, "Old Rocks Where They Shouldn't Be," CEN Technical Journal, Vol. 11, No. 3 (1997), pp. 257-258.

Cosmology

[129] Stephen Hawking, *A Brief History of Time*, New York: Bantam Books (2017), p. 42.

[130] Ibid, p. 41.

[131] Ibid, p. 122.

[132] Ibid, p. 201.

[133] Ibid. p. 45.

[134] Stephen W. Hawking and George F. R. Ellis, *The Large-Scale Structure of Space-Time*, Cambridge: The Cambridge University Press (1973), p. 134. Quoted in D. Russell Humphreys, *Starlight and Time*, Green Forest, AR: Master Books (1994).

[135] Stephen Hawking, *Brief Answers to the Big Questions*, op. cit., p. 28.

[136] Ibid, p. 38.

[137] Stephen Hawking, *A Brief History of Time*, op. cit., pp. 131-132, describing work of Alan Guth.

[138] Ibid, p. 136.

[139] Ibid, p. 201.

[140] Ibid, p. 48.

[141] Ibid, p. 210.

[142] Ibid, pp. 199-200.

[143] Russell Humphreys, "Our galaxy is the centre of the universe, 'quantized' red shifts show," *TJ*, Vol. 16, No. 2 (2002).

[144] Ibid.

[145] Russell Humphreys, "Creationist cosmologies explain the anomalous acceleration of Pioneer spacecraft," *Journal of Creation*, Vo. 21, No. 2 (2007), pp. 61-70.

[146] Russell Humphreys, "New time dilation helps creation cosmology," *Journal of Creation*, Vol. 22, No. 3 (2008), pp. 84-92.

[147] Russell Humphreys, "Biblical Evidence for Time Dilation in the Cosmos," *Creation Research Society Quarterly*, Vol. 53, Spring 2017, pp. 297-305.

[148] Russell Humphreys, "New view of gravity explains cosmic microwave background radiation," *Journal of Creation*, Vo. 23, No. 3 (2014), pp. 106-114.

[149] Ibid.

[150] See, for example, Hugh Ross, *Creation and Time*, Colorado Springs, CO: NavPress (1994), p. 9.

[151] Russell Humphreys, "The Creation of Cosmic Magnetic Fields," Proceedings of the Sixth International Conference on Creationism, Andrew Snelling, ed., Pittsburgh, PA: Creation Science Fellowship (2008), pp. 213-230.

[152] Russell Humphreys and Mark De Spain, *Earth's Mysterious Magnetism and that of other celestial orbs*, Chino Valley, AZ: Creation Research Society (2016), pp. 46-52.

[153] Russell Humphreys, "The Creation of Cosmic Magnetic Fields," op. cit.

[154] Ibid.

[155] Russell Humphreys, "Reversals of the Earth's magnetic field," Proceedings of the First International Conference on Creationism, R. Walsh, C.l. Brooks and R.S. Crowell, eds., Pittsburgh, PA: Creation Science Fellowship (1986), pp. 113-123.

[156] Russell Humphreys, "Physical Mechanism for reversals of the Earth's magnetic field during the flood," Proceedings of the Second International Conference on Creationism, Pittsburgh, PA: Creation Science Fellowship (1990), pp. 129-140.

[157] R. S. Coe and M. Prévot, "Evidence suggesting extremely rapid field variation during a geomagnetic reversal," *Earth and Planetary Science Letters*, Vol. 92, Nos. ¾ (1989), pp. 292-298.

[158] P. Camps, M. Prévot, and R.S. Coe, "Revisiting the initial sites of geomagnetic field impulses during the Steens Mountain polarity reversal, *Geophysics Journal International*, Vol. 123 (1995), pp. 484-506.

[159] N. A. Jarboe, R. S. Coe, and J. M. G. Glen, "Evidence from lava flows for complex polarity transitions: The new composite Steens Mountain reversal record," *Geophysical Journal International*, Vol. 186 (2011), pp. 580-602.

[160] G. A. Glatzmaier and P. A. Roberts, "A three-dimensional self-consistent computer simulation of a geomagnetic field reversal," *Nature*, Vol. 377 (1995), pp. 203-209.

161 Russell Humphreys, "Can Evolutionists Now Explain the Earth's Magnetic Field?," *Creation Research Society Quarterly*, Vol. 33, December 1996, pp. 185-186.

162 R. S. Coe, N. A. Jarboe, M. Le Goff, and N. Petersen, "Demise of the rapid-field-change hypothesis at Steens Mountain: The crucial role of continuous thermal demagnetization," *Earth and Planetary Science Letters*, Vol. 400 (2014), pp. 302-312.

163 Andrew Snelling, "More Evidence of Rapid Geomagnetic Reversals Confirms a Young Earth," *Answers in Depth*, Vol. 10, Jan. 8, 2015. Available at answersingenesis.org

Post Trial

164 David Down, "Searching for Moses," *TJ*, Vol. 15, No. 1 (2001), pp. 53-57.

Postscript

165 John Doane, "Spinoza's Ghost in the Evangelical Closet," *Creation Research Society Quarterly*, Vol. 59, No. 3 (2023), pp. 128-141.

INDEX

Want to connect with Dr. John Doane and explore more about his work?

Scan the QR code below to access exclusive content, updates, and insights!